THE SINGEF
RULE BOOK – 101 WAYS

TABLE OF CONTENTS

© 2018 LARRY BUTLER
DID IT MUSIC
http://www.diditmusic.com

INTRODUCTION

"You cannot knock on opportunity's door and not be ready."
- Bruno Mars

This book has taken over 40 years to write because that's about the length of time I've been in the live music performance arena – as a bar band musician, vocalist, songwriter, publisher, recording artist, road and tour manager, club and concert promoter, agent, major label VP in charge of touring, and personal manager.

Along the way, I took note of what **some performers** *did* to win over an audience and what **most performers** *didn't do* to fall short of that goal. And now I've taken those notes and experiences and attempted to put them into some kind of orderly and instructive fashion.

Although almost all of the **101 WAYS** pertain to contemporary music artists and performers of all types, the book is mainly addressed to the *solo singer/songwriter* because I've found that at the root of most popular musical performance combinations (duo/trio/quartet, rock bands and vocal groups) there is (or should be) a centerpiece figure – a leader – and generally that leader is also either the main songwriter or co-writer.

As you will see in the ensuing pages, in these rough economic times in the music business, one of the best ways to make a living is to be a self-contained singer/songwriter who owns the melody, the lyrics, the voice, the song arrangement and the recording. If you don't own and/or control all of those elements, you're at a disadvantage. Not that this book couldn't help you no matter how much of that profile matches your situation, but your ability to make a living at this will be diminished.

I can anticipate what you're thinking right now: "What can I learn from someone whose experience goes back 40 years? Everything has changed!" Actually, **the only thing that has changed** is the loss of the major income stream from record sales and the manner in which the audience is receiving and consuming recorded music. But as far as singer/songwriters and live performances are concerned, **how to ENTERTAIN an audience has not changed. The audience still wants to be entertained** no matter how well or badly the record business is doing.

Being a great solo singer/songwriter/performer/entertainer is probably **THE MOST DIFFICULT JOB IN THE ENTERTAINMENT FIELD TODAY** because it involves many skill sets, i.e., singing, songwriting, guitar and piano playing, story telling, stage presence and more. Each one of those requires learning a craft and transforming that craft into an art form. There are individual instructors available for all of those endeavors, but eventually you're going to need a live performance coach to pull those specialized skills together into a seamless, entertaining performance.

Before we begin, however, there are certain caveats.

Caveat 1: The **101 WAYS** that follow **are not guaranteed to make you a star**; they can only help you to improve your chances of success.

Caveat 2: These steps are designed to move your career from a *singer/songwriter/performer* to that of an *artist/writer/entertainer.*

Caveat 3: None of these instructions by themselves will change your life or your career. However, the more of them you adhere to, the better.

Caveat 4: Although the Table of Contents topic headings in which these **101 WAYS** appear may seem random, they're not. I've tried to arrange them in a step-by-step manner to build upon what's come before.

Caveat 5: It's not about who has the most talent; it's about who wants it more and will work harder to get it - the real secrets to success.

PERSONAL WAYS 1 -11

We're not going to jump right into the things you need to do to improve your live show or anything else related to music. First, we have to determine if you have the right mental attitude and physical well being to withstand the rigors of what lies before you.

So initially we're going to cover your dedication to your career, college and reading, sleep, diet and exercise, putting your body in peril for no reason, the pointlessness of mindless TV and sports fanaticism, dependable transportation, and keeping friends with benefits while distancing yourself from family, friends, relationships, pets, plants, and non-musical activities.

Many of these things you've heard before, but please do not push them aside or discredit them just because your mother mentioned some of these things to you at some point. Are you prepared to deal with the inevitable distractions that sway you from your path? How are you going to handle the constant tugs at your time from those who aren't helping? You need to prepare for this stuff, or all of your great songs will never be given the proper attention by the audience or the industry. All because you didn't utilize your time wisely.

#1 of 101 WAYS

Make sure that **MUSIC is the ONLY thing you want, need, and have to do in life** to the exclusion of everything else.

One thing for sure, from my experience of hobnobbing with successful (and some not so successful) rock stars for the past 40 years or so, no matter which goal they decided to pursue, the ones who focused on achieving just one goal, made it. **One goal, that's it, and nothing else.**

And they weren't just focused in the normal sense of working on something and then taking a break; nope, they were **SUPER FOCUSED.** No time off. Nothing else mattered. Not family, not friends, not loving relationships, nothing. If you weren't somehow related to helping them get to their one goal, you were in the way and did not matter.

Are you ready to do that, to be that person, to have that kind of focus? Are you ready to wake up each day and only engage in conversations and exchanges with those people and events that could further your career? **Are you ready to work on NOTHING ELSE but your career?**

If so, then read on! If not, then maybe you'd better prepare yourself for a life in something other than songwriting and performance. Why's that? Because **you will be competing for the attention of an audience with other artists who HAVE made that commitment.**

NOTE: This endeavor is not for those who just **WANT** to write songs and perform them in front of an audience in an entertaining manner. It's for those who **NEED** to do those things – they can't help themselves - they **HAVE** to do it – there are no other choices.

A cautionary note: **Do not have a back-up plan.** If you have "something to fall back on," you will end up doing that thing instead. **Make sure that this is all there is in life for you to do – singing, songwriting, performing, and entertaining**. And only do those things. Everything and everybody else is in second place.

Get as much of **a college education** as you can and **study the arts.**

The best way to study and learn about the arts, specifically music and literature, is in college, which will probably be the only four years of your life that will be fully-funded and, for the most part, unsupervised. No matter what, you should try to take advantage of that.

Great songs cannot be written without at least a semblance of what has come before in music and literature. Armed with the knowledge acquired studying the arts, you can then "borrow" from the classics at will.

Also, **an education forces you to think in rational terms** (so that you might become at least familiar with the concept) and helps you see the advantages of adding exposition, conflict, resolution and denouement to your songs – a beginning, middle, bridge and end, if you will.

Higher education strengthens your vocabulary and helps you speak well and convincingly, so that you can cajole others into doing something for you that perhaps they wouldn't have done if you weren't so persuasive.

Colleges have performance stages, radio stations, dance classes, theater groups, concert committees and more – all valuable assets for you to experience and utilize.

College broadens your worldview and permits you to see that perhaps there are more sides to the story than yours.

More than anything, it makes you READ - literature, history and poetry – all the elements of good stories and, hence, great songs.

#3 of 101 WAYS

Try to get
6 to 7 hours sleep
every night,
and by "night" I
mean somewhere
**between midnight
and 9 am.**

Even a tortured artist such as yourself must sleep. **The trouble is that most artists treat sleep as if it were some necessary evil. They don't fall asleep - they pass out. They don't wake up - they come to.**

If you're serious about being a successful artist/writer/entertainer, get out of that headspace of staying up late for no reason and sleeping the day away. Besides, that's not restful, restorative sleep. Sleep loss will affect your performance and, ultimately, your career. Here are ten good reasons not to lose sleep:

1. **Sleepiness causes accidents.** And not just in cars.
2. **Sleep loss dumbs you down.** And forget the myth about "catching up on sleep" – you can't - sleep doesn't really work that way.
3. **Sleep deprivation leads to serious health problems**. And you wonder why you're always getting sick?
4. **Lack of sleep kills sex drive.** This fact alone should make you reassess the value of sleep.
5. **Sleeplessness causes depression**. I know you think that it's cool to be depressed – it shows that you are a "true artist". Stop it.
6. **Lack of sleep ages your skin.** Deep sleep has a purpose – to restore and repair all your worn out body parts. Let it work.
7. **Sleepiness makes you forgetful.** You've probably been using the "no sleep" excuse a lot for not remembering to do stuff.
8. **Losing sleep can make you gain weight.** People who sleep less than six hours a night are 30% more likely to become obese than those who sleep seven to nine hours. Not fake news – actual fact.
9. **Sleep loss impairs judgment.** So when you're trying to evaluate your mental alertness and performance accurately, you can't! You haven't had enough sleep to do so!
10. **Lack of sleep increases the risk of death.** Besides, there's no guarantee your music will sell better just because you're dead.

Grow up and get some sleep.

Back off the nachos, beer and TV.
Eat a **low carb, high-protein diet and exercise** enough to keep the weight off.

You should do everything possible to look your best. Pursuing a career of performing (and entertaining) from a stage involves an audience staring at you for a half-hour or so every night.

You need to do some simple things every day in order to maintain the appearance of a somewhat healthy lifestyle. What we're talking about here are **not radical fad diets** – they take up way too much time and expense, which are resources that would be better spent on furthering your musical career.

Instead you should **concentrate on protein-rich foods**, the building blocks of good health, and **avoid the ever-present carbohydrates**. The trouble is carbs are everywhere and they taste so damn good and give you that quick, cheap energy boost, which is inevitably followed by the big energy crash. You know the one I'm talking about.

Exercise is mostly getting up off your butt and moving around. There's a lot to be said for treadmills, bicycles and standing desks, just as long as they're a means to an end and not life itself. **Be fanatic about your music career, not about your fitness schedule. Just do something!**

Your hands and your voice are your livelihood. No screaming! And stop playing amateur sports or doing any kind of repairs.

Your hands are big part of your audience visual communication package - the others being your mouth and your eyes – keep them safe! Avoid all amateur sports – basketball, volleyball, skiing, whatever – and all repair jobs. Let someone else help your uncle move his piano or fix his truck.

Now I guess that I'd be pretty remiss if I didn't at least say something about a major part of your singer/songwriter job – the singer part – **YOUR VOICE**. Although voice abuse is mainly in the realm of punk, hard rock, metal and the like, **losing one's voice through constant practice and the preponderance of notes at the high end of your range is not uncommon.**

However, as we'll touch on later, there is an element of entertainment in reaching for those high notes that you lose when you play it safe. So how do you do that without damaging the cords? You could meet with vocal coaches in your area and explain your situation. Do not work with anyone who tells you to stop trying to hit those high notes. It can be done with the correct training.

More about singing styles: You need to **DEVELOP A STYLE** to set yourself apart from the ones who either don't have the talent or don't want to take the time to learn. The ultimate goal is to have **TWO SINGING VOICES** – one for the up-tempo rockers and one for smooth ballads – don't just make the former louder than the latter. Examples of those who have or had that talent: Elvis, Elton, John Lennon, Chrissie Hynde, and Don Henley. I'm not aware of any contemporary artists who are exhibiting that talent – are you? Maybe it could be you! Get to work!

#6 of 101 WAYS

Avoid watching **mindless TV** or following **real or fantasy sports. Pointless.** They take up way too much of your precious time.

"How we spend our days, of course, is how we spend our lives."
— Annie Dillard

I'm actually writing this page of explanation about the downside of mindless TV and sports fanaticism on **Super Bowl Sunday 2017.** I'm aware of which two teams are playing — hard to get around that if you're monitoring the general news media — but I don't really care who wins because, with the possible exception of Lady Gaga and the lucky ones who had their songs placed in the commercials, **very few in the music community will financially benefit from this event. If anything, it sucks dollars out of the family entertainment budget that could have been better allotted to something musical instead.**

Note 1: If you'd rather pursue a career inside baseball or reality TV, then by all means, do so. Instead of practicing music, memorize the infield fly rule or marry a Kardashian.

Note 2: Should you decide to stop spending endless hours watching, following and discussing your favorite sports teams, there's no need to worry about any reaction from the team members themselves. They're probably not even aware that you've been a fan.

Note 3: The same goes for binge watching Netflix/Amazon or any other non-musical activity in which you may feel that you need to mindlessly indulge. I can't even begin to list how many other pointless activities that are out there, but I think you get the picture by now.

Of course, in order to justify your rabid sports fandom or TV addiction, **you rationalize that you deserve a break** from the rigors of musical practice and creativity. You think you need an outlet away from the music. But keep in mind that your competition isn't taking any breaks.

Do not listen to your family, friends or fans.

They're way too close to you to be objective about you, your music or your show.

OK, this is a common problem for every aspiring singer/songwriter – the well-intentioned family, friends and fans. Of course it's the way most everyone starts out. The parents buy the piano and guitar and pay for the lessons, and they are admiringly supportive of your efforts, even when you know you're not that good (yet) – but that's why you keep practicing.

Then the budding troubadour performs at parties. Friends, who never got past their first couple of lessons, are glad-handing you and pointing out how much better you're getting with every performance. After more practice and encouragement, you sign up for the school talent show and the whole school, teachers included, predict great things for you. Finally you're doing open mic nights and deservedly attracting a modicum of fans who know all ten of your songs note for note.

So now you think you're ready for the big time. **You're not.** It's time for a reality check. Your family, friends and fans, for all their genuine belief in you and your talent, don't know much about music or how to **ENTERTAIN** an audience. Even if they did, they're all way too close to you emotionally to make an accurate assessment of your music and your show.

You're going to need evaluation and instruction on the fine art of taking your well-honed **singer/songwriter/performer** skills and moving them up into the rarefied air of **artist/writer/entertainer**. Just the ability to write songs and accompany yourself as you sing them is not, in and of itself, all that entertaining.

If you were to learn how to actually ENTERTAIN an audience of complete strangers, then you would be able to separate yourself from that pack. That's what this RULE BOOK is all about.

#8 of 101 WAYS

Make sure you
**make friends,
some with
benefits
and some not,**
but all who want
to help you with
your career.

So here's where we separate the *singer/songwriter/performers* who are going to improve their chances of becoming successful *artist/writer/entertainers* from the ones who would rather be nice and allow people to run their lives for them. You need to lose the ones who do not come with the desire and dedication to help you with your career.

Here's how and why: As you're achieving some degree of notoriety as an artist with potential, the receiving line of people who want to be your "friend" starts getting longer and longer. And that's a good thing. So now you have a larger group of resources and talent to tap into to help you along the road to success. But there's wheat and there's chaff.

All I'm saying is that it would be beneficial and smart for you to assess this gene pool for the ones with common sense and passion for what you're doing musically and ASK FOR THEIR HELP. Unfortunately, among these followers will be what's known as "hangers-on" and they need to be gently, firmly and quickly thanked but no thanks. They'll slow you down. And that's the last thing you need right now.

There are numerous ways to go about this but I'll let your method fit your style. You are going to have to have a "tough love" script up your sleeve more often than not. Don't wait to use it. Make it clean and fast and move on.

Better yet, assign them "superfan" status online and **utilize their numbers to gain traction in social media**. It's a juggling act – but so is life.

Avoid marriage or any serious relationships.

Break-up with the live-in boy/girlfriend.

And there's no reason to have kids right away; everyone in your band will behave as if they're 12 years old anyway.

And here's another one that's going to get the haters up in arms. But come on, everyone who's ever been a performer knows that as soon as a significant other enters the picture, the career is put on hold. It's scriptural – you cannot serve two masters. **There can only be one driving force in your life – the pursuit of a career in music.**

You're looking for HELP in furthering your career, not HINDRANCE. It's OK to have a casual or friendly relationship - as long as it relieves tension instead of adding to your mounting list of fires to put out. And, inevitably, **relationships lead to unsolicited advice**. Reminder: you should not be taking any advice from anyone you are close to or emotionally involved with or whatever you want to call it. Only take advice from third party, unrelated professionals. You have to weigh the value of the relationship to the actual benefit. Relationships take time – do you have that kind of time?

Then there are kids. If you already have some, you have to stick with them and be a good parent. It is the only real responsibility you have in life. Do the right thing.

But, as headlined on the previous page, if you don't have kids and think you want some, hire or join a band. Since all musicians act as if they're 12 years old anyway, you can play out your parental role with them. Better idea: get a tour manager to do that.

NOTE: Being a tour manager is the worst job in the world – just in case you thought otherwise – but the reasons for which I say that are beyond the scope of this treatise. But trust me - I speak from experience.

Do not adopt any cats/dogs/plants or other high maintenance, non-musical responsibilities.

This instruction may actually be harder for some of you than losing family, lovers and unneeded friends – not having any pets or plants. But, let's face facts: pets are just short of kids in regards to the time and money spent to keep up the maintenance. The food, the walks, the clean-up's, the vet bills, and the accouterments are all drains on your time, your cash, and the part of your brain that should be focused, once again, on your music.

If, indeed, you **MUST** have some down time with an animal, offer to cat or dog sit for friends and neighbors while they're away. At least you'll be able to call on them for some awkward favor in the future.

Same thing with plants. They need daily care and, even then, they're going to die. Do not continue to live in the belief that somehow you're going to have a garden in your apartment. Nurture your songs instead.

FINAL WORDS ON THE SUBJECT: Unlike most legal agreements that try to cover every possible contingency, I'm not going to attempt to list all of the high maintenance, non-musical responsibilities that you may come up with that could sway your attention away from your goal. Lose them all. Now. Today. And let's get on with living your life for yourself and your career.

You do not have the time to waste. All of your clocks are ticking – musical, biological, and financial. So do it now!

Get large, cheap, low-mileage, **dependable transportation** so that your gear can be hidden and secured.

You will need a way to transport your gear, especially if you're playing piano and guitar through an amp and maybe carrying a small PA system on stands. And although you could probably figure out a way to get all of those things into a standard-sized car, but some of it wouldn't be hidden and therefore it would be unsecured.

If you must use a car, DO NOT leave any gear on back seats or within sight. Cover everything with dark colored blankets. Better yet, DO NOT leave ANY gear in your car at all.

If you're carrying more than just a guitar/keyboard/small amp (which should fit into a trunk), what you'll need is a van with no windows. It needs to run dependably and have relatively low mileage, but it should be a little old and beat-up to give the impression of being owned by someone with no visible means of support and might even be living in it.

DO NOT put any signage or logos or anything on your van to indicate that there might be valuable gear inside. It's an advertisement to break in and steal your gear.

Just to be on the safe side, have a welder construct a metal mesh screen between the front seats and the rest of the van, thereby providing a visual and physical deterrent to any unscrupulous passersby. Back the van up against a wall to prevent anyone from breaking into the back doors. Park it in a well-lit area. Put an alarm on all of the doors. Double-check the locks every time you leave it unattended.

And for God's sake, buy some gear insurance. See WAY #73.

MUSICAL

WAYS 12 - 19

Now that you've gotten your life together and your head on straight (thanks to the first **11 WAYS)**, we will begin the constructive musical and performance segments of **THE SINGER/SONGWRITER RULE BOOK.** Caution: If you don't address the initial **11 WAYS** first and foremost, the pursuit of your artist/writer/entertainer goals will all be for naught. You need to be prepared for what's to come.

Not that the next **90 WAYS** are going to be all that much fun. A lot of it is *unlearning some bad habits* you've picked up so far. Even more of it involves you learning (or re-learning) how to play and sing and perform and plan and practice and be (or maybe just appear to be) **PROFESSIONAL.**

This is work. How much work? As a rule of thumb, I tell clients that however long it's taken you to learn how to competently sing and play songs that you've written, that's how long it's going to take to move from being just a performer to being an actual, professional **ENTERTAINER.** Ready? Let's go!

Learn how to perform as **a solo artist**. There's way less overhead and you never have to attend any band meetings.

OK – the first thing you as a singer/songwriter must learn how to do is to perform solo. Why? In addition to being less expensive to mount a career (vis-à-vis a band), at every step along your uphill performance path, you are going to have to know how to perform and **ENTERTAIN** in some kind of **solo**, acoustic, stripped-down, bare bones situation, and sometimes at the drop of a hat.

Do you want to get radio airplay? You're going to have to physically go to every radio station in the US who might conceivably play your record and perform **solo** in conference rooms for the programmers, their staff and maybe some contest winners.

And it's the same thing to get the attention of music supervisors and ad agencies – you're going to have to set up in a **solo** acoustic setting and perform in office break rooms or at conventions and seminar showcases.

Your goal is to not only be **GREAT** at it, but to also be better than the singer/songwriter who was performing in their conference room the day before. Is your song that much better? Maybe. Is your show way more entertaining? It had better be or you lose out.

You can't be just good or even very good – you have to be GREAT!

Buy an inexpensive, tunable and playable **acoustic guitar with a very good pickup.** But learn to play on an electric guitar with headphones so you only bother yourself.

Old joke: A neighbor calls to ask a novice musician if he might borrow his guitar. The guitarist says, "I didn't know you could play guitar." The neighbor replies, "I can't. But while I have it, neither can you."

The idea here is to learn how to play guitar (and piano) adequately and competently enough to accompany yourself while singing your songs. There's no need to be the flashy player, **just learn how to play well enough to sell the song.**

Don't spend a lot of money on your first instrument. Besides, just because it costs more money doesn't make it a better instrument to play. For guitars, you'll need something tunable (that will stay tuned) and playable (with the strings comfortably close to the frets). An adjustable bridge would help with that string height.

The acoustic guitar needs to have a very good pickup – that makes all the difference in the world as to how it sounds through an amp or a DI (direct input) box. For learning and rehearsal purposes, you probably should use an electric guitar with headphones, especially if you have neighbors (and all the more reason to live alone – review **WAY #9**).

If you plan to at least initially use these instruments on stage, make sure that they're not flashy looking so as not to distract the attention of the audience away from you and your song. Brown wood acoustics and black electrics are fine. Avoid red, white, blue and all the other primary colors. Those would only work if the average age of your audience were 12.

#14 of 101 WAYS

Get a good
guitar chord book
(available online).
**Learn how to play
rhythm guitar well.**
You can hire a lead
guitar player later for
all the flashy stuff.

I would imagine any good chord book would do. Online chord instruction would probably help too. Even if you think you know everything there is to know about chords (you don't), go back and learn all the same chords in different fret positions.

The goal here is for you to master the art of rhythm guitar playing, with maybe a semi-flashy lead or two thrown in occasionally to make the audience believe that you really are a player. Again, don't waste your time pursuing a virtuoso (or virtuosa) level of playing.

The focus here is for you to be able to competently and professionally accompany yourself while singing your songs. The next step from there is to become a **great entertainer**. It's a big jump from the former to the latter, but you cannot make that leap without first mastering the former.

Get an inexpensive **61-key digital keyboard** that has several piano, B3-organ-with-Leslie, and synth presets.

You may want to get a teacher for this to avoid any bad habits.

For keyboards you don't need 88 keys – 61 will suffice, which is the fewest number I'm aware of that still features "weighted" keys with a piano action. You don't need hundreds of sounds – a few piano sounds and some basic B-3 organ and standard synth sounds will do for now. It should have real or simulated weighted keys.

To start, you could transfer the rhythm guitar chords you've learned onto your left hand, leaving the right hand available for contrapuntal melodies to augment your song's vocal melody. Or something along those lines.

To properly learn both the guitar and piano you should hire well-regarded teachers so that you don't pick up a lot of bad posture and fingering habits. Not hard to find these people – they're everywhere.

Go online or take
a class to learn
music theory,
chord progressions
and harmony, and
practice,
practice,
practice.

This is where some college courses would help (see **WAY #2**). Once you've cleared that initial hump of learning the right way to finger notes and basic chords on keyboards and guitar, you should seek out some sort of instruction on music theory, chord progressions and harmony.

Your goal is to be conversant and somewhat knowledgeable about those things, not only to be able to write chord progressions underneath your melodies, but also to be able to converse with actual musicians at some point. **If there's anything musicians hate most, it's working with or for someone who knows little to nothing about music, harmony and theory.** Don't freak out – it's not any different than any other profession, **all you really need to know is the jargon**. You can fake the rest.

#17 of 101 WAYS

Get a real nice set
of **headphones**
that you can wear
all day comfortably
to practice with.
DO NOT
blast out your ears.

Here are some facts about earphones, headphones and hearing loss. Today, **one in every five teens has some form of hearing loss** - a rate about 30% higher than it was in the 1980s and 1990s - which many experts believe is due, in part, to the increased use of headphones.

Most handheld players today can produce sounds up to 120 decibels, equivalent to a sound level at a rock concert. At that level, **hearing loss can occur after only about an hour and 15 minutes**.

If you can't hear anything going on around you when listening to headphones, **the decibel level is too high**. As a rule of thumb, you should only listen at levels up to 60% of maximum volume of the device or source for a total of 60 minutes a day. The louder the volume, the shorter your duration should be. At maximum volume, you should listen for only about five minutes a day.

The type of hearing loss due to headphone use is typically gradual, cumulative and without obvious warning signs. Unfortunately**, the type of hearing loss caused by overexposure to very loud noise is irreversible.**

As an alternative to earphones, you should consider using **older style, larger headphones that rest over the ear opening** instead of earphones that are placed directly in your ear.

Whether using headphones or earphones, **moderation is key**. Avoiding excessive use of listening devices altogether will go a long way in preventing hearing loss.

Bottom line: if you're going to pursue a career in music (an audio art), you should protect your own source of hearing. Losing the highs and lows of the audio spectrum will not serve you well in the future.

Work on learning how to sing and play at the same time **WITHOUT LOOKING** at your fretboard or keyboard.

This is going to take some time.

You need to be able to play without looking anywhere but at your audience. The goal here is far more than learning chords – it's the familiarity with your fretboard and keyboard. What we're aiming for is your eventual ability to play your songs all the way through without (or only occasionally) looking at your fretboard or keyboard. If you're constantly interrupting your visual communication with your audience because you either can't feel your way around your instrument or, worse, you've forgotten the next chord, then you're barely performing and you're certainly not entertaining. Having to constantly look at your fretboard or keyboard is a nervous and bad habit that is real hard to break. **Start now by learning how to play and test yourself constantly by not looking.**

NOTE: It's perfectly acceptable, in fact preferred, for you to look at your fretboard or keyboard when you are playing a *seemingly* difficult riff. You need to make it appear to be so difficult, in fact, that it requires you to turn away from looking at the audience and focus on your instrument.

This achieves two goals in the pursuit of entertaining an audience:
1) You are turning the audience's attention away from you singing your song to you playing a riff, thereby establishing a new visual.
2) You are showing the audience that, in addition to being a great singer/songwriter/performer, you *appear* to be an accomplished musician as well.

Of course, it would be best if the musical passage in question were actually *easy* to play, diminishing any fear that you might screw it up. **Since 90% of the audience has no musical experience, they won't know the difference. They'll have to take your word for it.** The visual of you intently focused on playing the supposed tricky riff tells them that it's difficult. Be sure to allow a few bars after the riff before you start to sing again, allowing time for a smattering of applause. Nod accordingly.

Get to the point
where you can sing
and play your songs
WITHOUT THINKING
about the
lyrics or chords
or anything else
but the audience.

Here's the path we're following, although I'm getting a little ahead of myself here:

1) Learn how to play (chords, progressions, theory) piano and guitar competently.
2) Practice playing until you don't have to look at the fretboard or keyboard all the time.
3) Learn classic singer/songwriter songs (next section).
4) Start writing your own songs (also next section).
5) Learn and practice playing and singing your own songs while looking directly at an audience and **without looking** at your keyboard, your fretboard, the ceiling or your shoes.
6) Get to the point where you can sing and play your own songs **without thinking** about the lyrics or chords or anything else but your audience.

All of this muscle memory comes from the now proverbial 10,000 hours of practice and performing.

The goal here is to have all of your focus on your audience as you're singing and playing your songs. It also frees you up to go to the emotion that you had when you first wrote the song and to tap into that thing that can't be faked. You can't go there while you're trying to remember the melody, lyrics and chords, let alone where you're going to move next, how the audience is reacting, or what you're doing after the show. **You want to get to that emotional core and it can't be done while your mind is everywhere else.**

This is the essence of performing and ultimately entertaining an audience.

SONGWRITING WAYS 20 - 28

OK, so we've gotten your personal life straightened out and we're to the point now that you can sing and accompany yourself on piano and/or guitar. It's time to work on the songwriting, because if you don't develop the ability and talent to write your own great songs, you're going to have trouble touting that you're a much of a singer/songwriter.

There is no one way to learn how to write songs, but there are certain conventions that songwriters use to make their songs more musical and more memorable. Melodies should have a chord progression underneath that flows fairly seamlessly to make the song sound "right". Your song's lyrics should fit into some sort of verse/chorus/bridge/chorus or similar format, again, to make the song musical and memorable.

What follows are some suggestions that you're probably not going to find in any other book on songwriting. These ideas relate specifically to your situation and the singer/songwriter genre. That's why they're here.

Great songs are really just three-minute stories, poems and plays set to music.

Get a free Kindle app. Download books onto a laptop, tablet or phone and **READ**
- preferably fiction and poetry. Take notes.

In order to write great songs, I mean REALLY great songs, you need a much larger worldview than whatever it is that you've been exposed to at home, at school, or among your peers. You have to **READ**. Read the classics. Read contemporary fiction. Read translations. Read.

In the current era where virtually all literature is a click away, there's no excuse not to. **And you don't need an actual Kindle tablet to take advantage of the Amazon library. Download the free app onto your computer, tablet or phone**. Instead of mindlessly keeping up with your "friends" on Facebook or wherever, you should be catching up on your reading anywhere, anytime.

Be sure to highlight and save the stuff that really touches you so that when you're done with a book, you'll be able to go back and re-read your highlights and maybe transfer the best stuff to a notebook or app. **All the great songwriters have some sort of notebook system.**

Not to discount melody as perhaps the major component of every great song, but you can't study melody as easily as you can lyrical content. **Melody is a gift; lyrics can be learned. Read.**

INSPIRATION: Back in **WAY #6** and in **WAY #10,** I tried in the nicest way possible to warn you about wasting time following sports, mindless TV, and all other high-maintenance, non-musical activities. However, there's a lot to be said about **the benefits of doing absolutely nothing** – clearing your mind in order to become aware and available when inspiration decides to strike. **Creativity relies on inspiration but you can't just make it happen**. It's great to daydream. Lie in bed for a while after you wake up and let your mind wander. Go for long walks in large parks with few distractions. Try to put the troubles of your everyday existence out of your head for a while. See what happens. Be sure to keep your muted cell phone or a pen and some paper within reach. You're going to need them.

#21 of 101 WAYS

Get a **Beatles songbook**. **Learn everything in it**.

Write a dozen songs "borrowing" from them.

When completed, **throw them away** and **start writing your own**.

No one has done the singer/songwriter thing better than the Beatles. Virtually every one of their songs can be reproduced by one voice with a piano or guitar because that's they way they were written.

The best part is that their stuff is all over the map. The remarkable thing about the Beatles output, in addition to all the hits, was that very few songs sounded a whole lot alike. They "borrowed" from a wide variety of musical styles and incorporated it all into a contemporary format.

What I'm getting at here is not another homage to the Beatles, but rather what a great treasure trove of diverse material for you as a budding, aspiring singer/songwriter to dive into and learn virtually everything you will need to know to start writing your own songs.

But first you need to immerse yourself into the Beatles songbook. The most complete, least expensive book I can find is $15 on Kindle (link below). It is arranged for solo singer/songwriters. That's you!
https://www.amazon.com/Beatles-Complete-Chord-Songbookebook/dp/B002TOJHCM/ref=tmm_kin_swatch_0?_encoding=UTF8&qid=&sr=
It doesn't include the instrumental riffs or background harmonies, but you should be able to work them out. If you can't, get a teacher. These songs are the fundamental building blocks of songwriting all in one place. Take advantage of your good fortune to have this available to you for $15. Get the Kindle version, not the paperback.

Step Two: Take what you learned from the Beatles and write a dozen songs utilizing stolen bits of melody, lyric and their inventive chord progressions. It doesn't matter how close you get to their originals, because when you're done, you're going to delete them and start writing your own songs. **Where would John, Paul and George have gone next if they could have put up with each other? That's your mindset.**

Write up-tempo songs or slow ballads only.

There are already way too many boring, boring, mid-tempo songs.

A goodly part of these **101 WAYS** will be spent on alerting you to some of the pitfalls and pratfalls I've witnessed in my years of observing singer/songwriter/performers in their natural habitat. **Without even hearing your first batch of songs I know that they're primarily mid-tempo.** Perhaps you've come up with a couple of up-tempo numbers and a few slow ballads, but it's a natural tendency for new songwriters to do their initial creative work sitting on a bed or sofa strumming away and hoping not to upset the family, roommates or neighbors. So by default, they write nice, pleasant, unremarkable, mid-tempo songs, fraught, of course, with heartfelt and personal observations about love, life and loss. Lovely, but boring, boring, boring.

Your first goal as a singer/songwriter is not to write the best song ever; you must first write songs that will win over audiences made up of uninterested strangers or, worse, jaded professionals. You need a plethora of up-tempo, hard-driving, bouncy rockers. The idea is to get people to **FIRST FEEL your songs, and THEN they'll start to LISTEN.** That cannot be accomplished with mid-tempo songs. **You will also need a couple of slow, tearful, power ballads to show your audience that you wear your heart and your emotions on both sleeves.**

NOTE: This is not to take anything away from the value of your heartfelt, clever, emotional mid-tempo songs at all. But from a **TEMPO** and **VISUAL** perspective, they aren't going to get the same reaction as up and down tempo songs from an audience who is unfamiliar with you. Later on, once you've won over audiences and they are bringing others back to see you, you can start including your mid-tempo songs in the set. Not before.

OK, ANOTHER NOTE: Mid-tempo songs are **GREAT** for songwriter rounds. That's when three-to-five songwriters get together and play maybe four songs, one at a time. In fact, mid-tempo songs are practically required for such events.

FINAL NOTE: Up-tempo song tip: **Everybody loves a shuffle.**

Use as many
one-syllable words
as possible.

They're easier for
the audience to
understand and
to remember.

The idea that it's easier to learn a song if there is a preponderance of single syllable words in it seems pretty straight forward, right? But taking it one step further, **I believe that the success of English as the *lingua franca* of global popular music is all due to one attribute: the abundance of single syllable words. They make the song easier to sing, to rhyme, to set to meter and, most of all, to remember**. So when writing song lyrics, given the plethora of word choices in English that all mean the same thing, more than likely one of the word choices for the lyric would be a single syllable word, and so, by default, that word would be the best to use in the song.

As a for instance, Sam Hunt's "Body Like A Back Road" (as written by Sam with Shane McAnally, Josh Osborne and Zach Crowell) has six stanzas containing a total of 255 words, by my rough count; 225 (or 88%) of them are single syllable words and the remaining 30 (or 12%) have two or more syllables. 88% is a lot! Compare that to your own songs.

NOTE: The song broke a record for the most consecutive weeks at #1 on the *Billboard* Hot Country Song chart (34) and was the best selling country song of 2017. Apparently people liked hearing it multiple times.

Now I haven't done a word-for-word translation of this song with other languages, but my experience with French, Spanish and German in high school was that there just aren't that many single syllable words in the other major Western languages. Perhaps there's some Polynesian dialect spoken on some faraway South Pacific atoll made up of only single syllable words, but they aren't teaching it in Ohio and nobody's buying their records. Only in English could such a feat be accomplished. And that's what makes a song instantly and easily more memorable.

NOTE: Along those same lines, **FEWER** words in each line would help an unfamiliar audience remember your song on a first listen as well.

The audience does not want to hear all that much about **YOUR** life – they want to hear about **THEIRS.**

"The easiest songs to write are pure fiction. There is no limit to how you can tell the story." – Jason Mraz

In order to start to make your mark in the singer/songwriter field, you're going to have to learn how to successfully **ENTERTAIN** a bunch of strangers in the dark space of a small club. You have to start somewhere.

We've already discussed the need for up-tempo songs with an occasional slow ballad thrown in so that they (and you) can catch your collective breaths. Now let's talk about the mood of the average club goer. (Forget about your family and friends – they're not the ones you're trying to win over.)

I don't believe that the average club audience member is exuberantly happy or clinically depressed. The former would be doing something other than sitting around a small club waiting to watch and listen to an unknown singer/songwriter/performer, and the latter would be home in bed eating ice cream and watching old black and white movies on Netflix.

So your songs need to address the problems and solutions of being not real happy and not real sad. Let them know that you've been there. Tell them that you were real happy or real sad in the past but now you're somewhere in between. So sing about what happened to those high or low spots in your life, and how you're coping with your life now, which should shed some light on how they might cope with theirs. These are universal themes to address.

The lyrics can be from personal experience, even with some specifics thrown in, but make sure that they're relatable to a wider audience. **Better yet, as Jason Mraz says above, make it up.**

Make sure that your songs contain **all four ways to ENTERTAIN an audience** – melody, lyrics, tempo, and a catchy opening riff.

We've already covered the need for up-tempo songs. Next: **Melody or Lyrics – which comes first?** There are many and varied differences of opinion on that question. Let's consult the stars:

Bob Dylan – *"I consider myself a poet first and a musician second."*
Max Martin – *"Writing the melody first gives me more freedom than doing it the other way around."*
Joni Mitchell – *"It's not a good song until it has a lyrical sensitivity and a moment of clarity. Until then, it's just complaining."*
Don Henley – *"Sometimes songwriters and singers get a melody in their heads and the notes will take precedence, so that they wind up forcing words onto a melody. It doesn't ring true."*
Alison Krauss – *"Lyrics are the whole thing. Even with a great melody, if you're not singing the truth, it doesn't work."*
Steven Tyler – *"Great melody over great riffs, that's the secret of it all."*
Sia – *"Melody comes first and then I have to choose lyrical content that feels aligned to that."*
And, from all reports, **Lennon and McCartney** preferred melody first.

Opening riff: How many times have you sat through eight or (worse) 16 bars of the opening of a song that was just a chord or two strummed repetitiously, which would gradually mesmerize you into a semi-soporific state, thereby causing you to not care about the song at all by the time the performer got around to singing the opening lines? **If you're not moving around the stage and attempting to make eye contact with the audience, quit the pointless strumming and start the song!**

Sorry, but again we must refer back to the Beatles' repertoire. Almost all of their songs have a catchy opening riff. Or they would limit the opening strum to either two or four bars. Or if they couldn't come up with anything, they'd do a cold open. You should remember to pull that out of your songwriting toolbox when faced with a similar dilemma.

Your songs must hold up with **just your vocal and one instrument. Your delivery is key.**

Any need for additional voices or instruments is just an excuse to cover up a mediocre song.

"If you can't sell your song while standing under one light bulb and singing into one microphone while accompanied by one guitar, then you're not a performer and it's not a song." – David Lee Roth

Leave it to Diamond Dave to put everyone straight on that subject. The **strength of the song is the first factor** in the quality evaluation test.

The second factor is selling the song and that's all about the delivery. You have to find the soul of the song and deliver the emotional feeling behind it. A great song will always be a great song, but if the singer who delivers it is just OK but not really great, most of the potential audience will miss the conveyance of that feeling.

It's the artistry of the songwriter combined with the artistry of the singer that make the song entertaining and great. That's why, when you hear the demo of your favorite song sung by either the original author or some demo singer, it may not work as well as the song in the hands of a real song stylist. The ones who took the first shots weren't necessarily the best interpreters of the song. The same goes for when other artists cover great renditions of great songs, many times it falls flat.

So the burden is really on the shoulders of the singer/songwriter to not only write a great song, but also to sing it with all the poignancy required to get it across to an audience. Your song isn't finished until you have discovered the way to accomplish that every time you sing that song.

Are you ready for that? I don't think so - not yet. But it's a goal to keep in mind. Better read on.

You needn't suffer from **Songwriter Writer's Block** any longer. Here's why.

Most experts agree that there's no reason anyone should suffer from Songwriter Writer's Block for the simple reason that it doesn't exist! Great songwriting comes from inspiration but inspiration comes and goes as it pleases. So then it's just a matter of what to do while you're waiting.

YOU HAVE TO BE READY TO CAPTURE INSPIRATION THE MOMENT IT'S PRESENTED OR ELSE IT GOES OFF INTO THE ETHER. So it's important to keep working regardless. It would be truly beneficial if you were sitting at your keyboard (computer or piano) when inspiration decides to fly by.

Here are ten things you could be doing to while you're waiting:
1) Write a song from someone else's perspective rather than yours.
2) Change instruments – try writing a melody using a kalimba!
3) Write in the style of a known artist and not necessarily one that you admire.
4) Write down your fears or who you're mad at and why. That should be easy. Is there a song of acceptance or tolerance there?
5) Start with the ending and work backwards, but make the ending a complete surprise – a twist – and not what anyone would expect.
6) Scroll through the plot synopses in Rotten Tomatoes for ideas.
7) Open a book and write about the first word or phrase you see.
8) Turn on the TV and write about the first thing you see and hear, even if it's an infomercial for a timeshare.
9) Open up Spotify, close your eyes, and keep tapping the screen until a song starts to play. Transcribe that melody. Then play it backwards. Repeat that process until you find a melody you like.
10) Print out the names of as many chords as you can from your online chord book. Cut them up and put them all into a bowl. Pick some randomly and devise weird chord progressions from them.

Yes, these could take some time to do, but time is something you've got plenty of while you're waiting for inspiration to fly by. Be ready!

Once you've finished a song, **move it up a couple of keys.** It will add power and emotion to your live performance.

There are two things about your song to which an unfamiliar audience is going to initially respond, and your song itself isn't one of them. Sorry. The first thing is what we just went over in **WAY #22** - tempo – make it fast or slow it down.

The second thing is the emotional message that you bring to the song. **You want to show an audience that you really believe in your song, so much so that you can't contain your emotions in the delivery.** One way to accomplish that is for your voice to quiver and crack and stretch and strain to indicate the emotion behind the lyric. The best way to do that is to merely move the song up a couple keys. **Get it out of the comfortable key you chose when you wrote it in your bedroom** and move it into a place where you're going to have trouble reaching the high notes.

The physical thing your voice has to do as you try to reach those notes will be reflected in your face and body language. You're going to have to move away from the mic, **lean back** and yell or scream to get into that upper register. From the standpoint of the audience, that combination of vocal extremes and visual discomfort will subliminally show them how much the song means to you (real or not) and they will respond accordingly.

You will have to leave your current performance comfort zone to pull this off, but that will be yet another sign of how you're moving your live act from just performing to **a real emotional connection with your audience – and that's entertaining!**

#29 of 101 WAYS

RECORDING

Now that you can sing and play your own songs, you think it's time to record an album.

IT'S NOT.

For some (or possibly/probably most) of you, it's all about recording. You want to have some tangible thing to show off to your admiring friends and family and to flaunt in front of the naysayers - "Hey look! I made an album!" But today, virtually anyone can make an album. And the singer/songwriters who record and release albums too soon in their careers end up being embarrassed by them years later because they weren't really ready.

So we actually have two problems here:
1) **Albums are over – a waste of time and money. These days smart artists only release singles consistently over time.**
2) **You're not ready to release any music yet regardless.**

I know these admonishments won't stop most of you. **Go ahead – spend all of that money and waste all of that time recording an album when you should be concentrating on your live show.** When you're done and the initial thrill is over and nothing has happened with your album-length CD, we'll start up again where we left off in making your live show better.

After all, what is a recording but the live performance of a song captured in time by electronics? So doesn't it stand to reason that if your live show is not the best it can be yet, you should not be recording anything less than great songs sung by a seasoned performer?

Even if you have an album already made, NO credible manager, agent, record company, publisher, investor, or whoever will be interested in you or your songs until they have they seen how well you can play live and if you have a growing live audience. Live comes first.

And yet there are a couple of things that you can do to educate yourself about recording so you can get some self-produced trial demos together.

Get to know
your way around
Garage Band
and the basics of
Pro-Tools.
Befriend a trained
audio engineer
for your demos
and live shows.

Here's where you start building your team.* The most immediate slot you need to fill is someone to help you with the technical and logistical aspects of your live show. You'll need an **audio engineer** to take over the sound reproduction of your vocals and instruments, both in demo sessions and on stage. And if this **audio engineer** also happens to know his or her way around guitar and piano, you are golden.

With the help of your newfound **audio engineer** friend, start to record your rehearsals and shows. Later, play them back to critique with your engineer. **DO NOT** play them back for family and friends (yet) and, above all, your fans. **DO NOT** allow anyone to have copies. **DO NOT** let anyone convince you to post any of your live stuff anywhere. It's not good enough (yet). And once it's up online, it lives **FOREVER** and you will **FOREVER** regret doing that.

NEXT, the two of you should start to utilize what you've learned from listening back to your rehearsals and shows and maybe begin work on some demos of the four or five songs that are the closest to being done. No matter what you think, they're not done yet, but putting them down in demo form should reveal that fact to you both and give you a starting point toward eventually recording them properly.

*Of course eventually you'll need a manager, tour manager, agent, PR rep, merch person, social media maven, etc. But you can start now by building your team, one person at a time.

Get a **MacBook Pro** with as much memory as you can afford to record and store all of your demos, rehearsals, photos, videos and shows.

Back it all up frequently to an external hard drive, flash drive, cloud storage – or all three!

Life is maintenance. The more maintenance you do, the better your life is going to be. Maintenance is also a pain in the ass. It never stops needing to be done.

Organization requires maintenance. Anyone can **GET** organized; the trick is to **STAY** organized and to **MAINTAIN** the organization you've set up. It really doesn't matter **HOW** your system works, only that it **DOES** work. The "organizers" available in stores or online are only useful to those who are already organized. Those things cannot take the place of the daily maintenance of your system.

And that brings us to how well you're going to organize and maintain your inventory of demos, rehearsals, photos, videos and shows.

1) You will need to input as much metadata as you can into the Info section of each file. Don't put it off – you'll either never come back to it or, if you do, you will have forgotten what it was about.

2) Back up everything to an external hard drive/flash drive/cloud – frequently or, preferably, constantly.

3) Do not rely on someone else to do any of this. It's tedious and boring at the same time. You're the only one who has the need to get it done. Sorry.

VISUAL & STYLE WAYS 32 – 38

OK, so you've been focusing these last few weeks/months (perhaps years) on your songs, your voice, your guitar and piano playing – all of the things related to the *audio* portion of your live show. But the word *show* denotes a visual element, so we're going to devote pretty much the next third of this book to just that – *the visual.* The visual will comprise most of the ways in which we are going to transform the live *audio* performance reproduction of your songs into an entertaining *visual* live show.

We're going to start with the obvious parts of the visual aspect of your presentation, which should be the easy fixes when compared to what follows. And it could be the fun part as well.

We're going to touch on hairstyles (or lack thereof), headshots, stylists and shopping, wardrobe tips, a logo, video treatments of your songs and a word of caution about video production projected times and costs. Ready?

Create a
hairstyle that is
one step away
from a normal look
- **not two steps** -
or get a distinctive,
but non-gaudy hat.

FIRST IMPRESSIONS: It usually takes maybe ten seconds or so to enter a stage and get to the mic before you start to sing. Now, at least half of the audience is going to decide if they like you or not in that first ten seconds, mainly based on how you entered the stage and approached the mic, the look or lack of confidence on your face, *and your hairstyle.* More than clothing and shoes, **hairstyle is the first thing the audience is going to notice about your look** – and to a live audience, *your look is initially more important than your songs.*

First, you need to decide if your hair is going to be a distinguishing trademark for you or not. I say yes, with a few caveats. The idea is not unlike the approach to your music. You should combine all of your influences with whatever is happening now, and come up with something one step away from what the audience knows and has accepted. **NOT TWO STEPS away from the norm, JUST ONE.** The audience cannot handle anything too far removed from what they've already accepted as OK ("What the hell is that?"); but they just might be curious about someone who's taken whatever is out there and moved it forward one step.

Boring hair is not an option. Either do something with it or cover it up. Now, if your hair, or lack of it, does not lend itself to a style or you can't quite settle on a look yet, maybe it's time for a hat, headband, or flower while you're waiting for inspiration to appear.

The first time a potential fan might see you or your headshot, you need to have an unforgettable look. That way when they come across you or your photo again, they'll remember you right away. Your hair doesn't have to look "fabulous" – but it has to be **UNIQUE** and it has to be **YOU!**

VERY IMPORTANT: For God's sake, figure out some way to style or hold back your hair so you don't spend the entire time on stage pulling it out of your face. It's very distracting and does nothing to enhance your show.

Get several B&W and color **headshots** with three different looks – **smiling, serious and sexy.**

First practice various expressions and profiles with selfies.

MY SEVEN STEPS TO A GREAT PHOTO SHOOT

1) **Headshots! Headshots! Headshots!** How many times must I repeat that before it sinks in? The only visual the audience needs upon their first introduction to you is a headshot. Long shots and fashion shoots only exist to keep photographers and stylists in business. **You only need headshots right now - horizontal/vertical and color/B&W.**

2) **Don't worry about what to wear.** Just simple, solid color tops. We're only interested in your face (mouth and eyes) and that fetching new hairstyle.

3) **You need to practice the three looks above (smiling, serious, and sexy) using only your mouth and eyes.** Take a variety of selfies and print them out for review. At first your expressions will seem stilted, silly and contrived. Keep practicing until your expressions seem genuine and natural. **Do not do a photo shoot until you're comfortable with your looks.** Only ask opinions about your selfies from trusted members of the opposite sex (perhaps a contradiction in terms) and not, once again, your family, friends and fans - they're too close to you, so they don't count.

4) **Do not do any outdoor shoots. Screw natural light. We don't want real – we want fabulous. And the only way to look fabulous is with great indoor professional lighting.**

5) **Find at least three professional photographers** (young or old, doesn't matter) in your town (they're everywhere). This is something where you shouldn't rely on some friend or a friend of a friend, but rather a recommendation of a professional from someone who knows what they're talking about.

6) **Set up interviews with the ones who seem viable and in your price range.** Make sure he or she does both film and digital and is an expert on various styles of interior lighting. **Interior lighting is everything.**

7) **Look through their portfolios and discuss their previous work with them.** Ask about whom they use for makeup. Go over the points above and say something about how you want to take this shoot a step further than the norm. Get a feel for your rapport with them – that's important.

Befriend someone
of the opposite sex
who has a
**tasteful, classic
fashion style.**
Take him or her
thrift store
shopping.

Now that your headshots are done, it's time to bring a stylist into the picture to start to develop a "look" for the live show (not for the headshot photo shoot - only for the stage). **DO NOT** have this person involved before you do the photo shoot – they will **INSIST** that you need to wear all kinds of wild, colorful, *fashionista* outfits in order to get "the look" for your photos. Headshots are the bane of every stylist – there's nothing for them to do! **You are NOT doing a fashion shoot;** so avoid having the headshot photo discussion with anyone who purports to be a stylist.

A stylist does need to be a part of your team though for your stage look. Unfortunately, you can't pay them anything yet. The whole look and style of photo shoots and stage wear will be re-examined and revised once someone comes along with the financial backing for you to move up to that level.

For the time being, you need to sweet talk your team into working with you with the serious intention of utilizing them when there's funding.

#35 of 101 WAYS

On stage, wear only **tasteful, solid-color clothing and little to no skin.**

Keep the focus on **your face and hands.**

No distractions!

It would be beneficial if you already have some ideas as to how you want to look or at least how you *don't* want to look. Here are some points I need to make in the interests of practicality.

1) Whatever it is you're going to wear on stage, it cannot distract from your face, hair and hands.

2) Keep it simple. You can't go wrong with solid dark colors. Stay away from greens – they're too hard to match. Make sure the colors complement (or at least don't clash with) your hair (or hat).

3) Ladies - Keep the skin to a minimum. Guys too, I guess. The only skin you want to show is your face and hands. More on that later in **WAY #44**.

4) Unless you can dance like Michael Jackson, there's no reason to draw attention to your socks or shoes. All footwear should be inconspicuous but should lend itself to the ease of walking and some simple steps (and running, should there be a fight or a fire).

5) Make sure that your stage clothes (and shoes) are lightweight and fit a little loosely. It gets REAL HOT on stage and you're going to be on your feet probably the whole time.

6) Put together a style that utilizes clothing that can be bought at thrift stores and can be washed out in a sink if need be. Your high fashion comes later when you can afford it.

With all of that in mind and having discussed it beforehand with your new best friend the stylist, get busy.

**Design a logo
of your name**

in both vertical and
horizontal formats.

Make sure they can
be read easily from
at least 20 feet away.

In addition to headshots to satiate the public's need for a visual, there's an equal need for a visual representation of your name – a logo.

I am the last guy you would want to consult with on anything regarding logos and graphics and artwork and such. Creative graphics are not my forte. I have ideas and opinions about such things, but I find the whole area to be entirely subjective, artsy-fartsy, and in the eye of the beholder. So I stay out of it.

However, I do have some practical tips to keep in mind, of course.
1) A logo needs to represent who you are as a person and an entertainer.
2) It needs to be simple and understandable and readable from 20 feet away when on a banner or a piece of merch. Don't make it so confusing or obscure so as to elicit comments like, "What the hell does that say?" Why alienate an audience? (Unless confusion, obscurity and alienation are what you're about.)
3) Make sure that the logo can be re-configured in a vertical, horizontal and even a square format. You never know.
4) Make sure that it works in color and in black and white.
5) Use line art - no halftones – too expensive to reproduce.

That's all I got for now. Get it done.

Create and write inexpensive **video ideas or treatments** for your songs.

Make friends with a **videographer.**

What's with all this Visual and Style stuff? Isn't it all about the music? Oh, yes, it's very much all about the music. None of the visual and style stuff means anything without the music. The music has to be created and performed first – no doubt. But it's the visual that captures the audience.

Here's a timely analogy: Think of your song as the cake and the visual and the style are the icing and decorations. You can go ahead and bake the best cake there can be and enter it into the Top Chef Baking competition. But my guess is, without the icing and decorations on top, you're not going to take home the Golden Spoon or whatever. And that's what you're faced with in the music biz today. **It's equal parts – it's an audio *and* a visual world – and you need both to be an ENTERTAINER.**

You should already have ideas about videos for almost all of your songs; preferably realistic, affordable ideas, but fully formed ideas nonetheless. They can be a mix of lyric, live or concept – even animated, although I'm pretty sure CGI/anime is very expensive.

Even better, those ideas should be storyboarded and presented to someone who does music videos professionally for viability and budget. God forbid that one of your songs gets noticed and placed and you aren't prepared with a video treatment, a proposal or a budget.

Of course, you're going to have to make friends with a videographer and add that person to your team with the promise of future work. Maybe you can muster up enough funding just to have something done for your current best song, just for the experience of having it done. I recommend a lyric video because your live performance isn't ready for prime time quite yet. You'll learn a lot. Do something visual. Go on. Do it.

Whenever you get a video production schedule and proposed budget, **double the time and the costs.**

VIDEO PRODUCTION PLANNING, TIMELINE AND ONE BIG TIP

When it comes time in the future to have a proper live action video done for one of your songs, first get a storyboard, a proposal, a budget and a shoot schedule and go over it with the producer, director, DP, everyone involved. Make sure that the editing and re-editing and color correcting and whatever else are all included in the proposal - turn key – all in. Then double all the costs in the budget and all the times allotted for the shoot and editing no matter what they tell you beforehand.

If the producer and director insist that their proposed costs and times are correct, add an addendum clause to your agreement holding them to those figures and times and that you will not pay for any overages. That may get them to rethink their proposal.

Because afterwards, trust me, there will be a plethora of excuses as to why it ended up costing twice as much and why the shoot took twice as long as they had predicted. There will be faulty equipment, staff no-shows, the weather, no permits - all semi-legitimate reasons/excuses, I guess, but still longer and more costly than you were promised.

It always happens. Double it. Learn it now or learn it later.

STAGING & PERFORMANCE WAYS 39 – 61

OK, this section is **the most important part of your path to an entertaining live show**. These are not weekend quick fixes; these ideas all take thought, planning, practice and execution in order to get to the point where it will seem as if they've always been there.

This section includes how to get comfortable on stage, what you can learn from watching concerts on TV and national touring acts in town, getting in good with local club bookers and production staff, having your own microphone and some mic technique tips, the need for rehearsal video and a movement coach, learning the song vs. rehearsing the song, rearranging songs for the live show, set lists and lengths, the need for entertaining stories and patter as well as stage personality and attitude, connecting with your audience through visual cues, and how to not allow your ego/pride to get in the way of revealing yourself and your songs to your audience from the stage.

**Build a mini-stage
wherever you can**
with hot lights,
a cheap PA,
and a floor-to-ceiling
mirror across the
opposite wall.

**Spend time there and
get comfortable.**

Staging and Performance – OK, here we go! Here's another thing that will separate you from the other singer/songwriter/performers out there.

The first thing you need to do is to learn to be comfortable on stage. Nothing turns off an audience more than when they detect that you are lost or scared or don't know what to do next. You're squinting under the lights, trying to talk to an audience you can't see, and you're blowing into the mic to determine if it's on or not because you apparently can't hear yourself. Your amp's not turned on or you're not plugged into the DI box correctly. Now the audience is unsure that you have the experience and confidence to put on an entertaining show. **The best way to show that confidence is to actually BE comfortable on stage.**

Now wouldn't it make sense to rehearse under the exact same conditions as you're going to experience on stage, except without an audience to judge you? But how, without running up a big bill at the local rehearsal space? Answer: **Build a small stage where you live or in a friend's garage** – that would be a friend with a benefit, as per **WAY #8**.

The whole idea is for you to get comfortable being on stage as early in your career as possible. We're not talking about just a practice space floor, but rather a fairly decent reproduction of a small club stage, maybe 16'x8'x2'. And be sure to have low-slung hot lights and a couple of old, beat up, single mix monitors, because that's what your gigs are going to be like in the first year or two of performing. Might as well get used to it.

If you always practice and rehearse like this, you should become way more comfortable and confident when you're actually on a real stage in front of an audience under similar conditions.

Get a cable TV package that includes **MTV Live** and/or **AXS TV** to watch live concerts for entertaining performance ideas.

Take notes. Steal.

Although the TV/Internet landscape keeps changing, there are two cable channels right now that I'm aware of that are showing full concert live performances (MTV Live and AXS TV) and there are any number of them on YouTube as well with varying degrees of age and quality.

But who's to say what's entertaining or not? If you're 20 to 30 minutes into the concert and you're losing interest, there's a lesson learned right there. Most experienced performers can keep an audience interested about that long – 20 to 30 minutes. But if nothing different is happening visually, it doesn't matter how great the players are and, to a certain extent, how great the songs are. An audience needs to be entertained visually.

I'm sounding like a stuck record, aren't I? Does anyone know what a stuck record sounds like anymore? I'm hoping that the recent vinyl resurgence helps bring that useful phrase back into vogue.

Keep a running list of shows in your area and try to see as many **national touring acts** as you can afford. Watch and listen for what they do between songs.

When I was first starting out playing in bands in high school in Centerville, Ohio, there were no opportunities to see seasoned bands perform in order to pick up some ideas of how to act on stage because very few national acts toured through our town or nearby Dayton. So we all got fake ID's and went to bars (some things never change).

But we found most bar bands to be boring. So we watched Marx Brothers movies on TV and stole routines from them. We listened to live concert records to hear patter and copied from them. We stole from whatever we could find. You should too.

It was only when we went off to college that we were able to go see major acts on a regular basis. That would be all the more reason for you to get out of your hometown and enroll in a big city college.

#42 of 101 WAYS

Get a list of all of the **club bookers** in your area. Start hanging out at their clubs and introduce yourself to them. **Be nice.**

You gotta start somewhere. **There are probably open mic nights where you live. I'm sure there are clubs who will allow you a slot if you can produce 10-15 paying customers**. Better make sure you've rehearsed the hell out of your show before you start putting the arm on friends and family — you're going to need them to tell others about you and bring them to the next show. Unless you're entertaining, that may not happen.

If possible, try to find places where they're not serving food at the same time as you're performing, although Norah Jones says she learned everything she knows about singing and playing at the same time from a regular restaurant gig she had outside of Dallas while in college. The patrons didn't pay much attention to her while they were eating, which allowed her to practice and hone her craft without having to actually rely on paying customers. Good gig!

Look for off nights to start with. Approach club bookers in person at the venues and ask about that. Punk rock reportedly took hold in New York in the mid-'70s when Tom Verlaine proposed to club owner Hilly Kristal that Tom's band Television should take over the slow Monday nights at CBGBs (aka Country Blue Grass Bar) in the Bowery for the door and Hilly would keep the bar. New York is always looking for the new hip thing and, as it happened, punk was new. In a month or so, CBGBs was featuring the Talking Heads, the Ramones and Blondie. Use that as inspiration to get your live show off the ground, even at places that wouldn't normally cater to your style of music.

Get your own vocal mic. God knows where the club's mic's have been.

Get a Shure Beta 58A. It's a supercardioid dynamic mic that you can **SING OVER THE TOP OF*** instead of directly into.

No more eating the mic.

*See next page for HOW

Most clubs and sound companies use Shure SM58's for vocals – they're the standard of the industry. Their sound reproduction is good throughout the vocal spectrum and, more importantly, they're cheap and you can "drop them" regularly onto the stage floor and they still work.

The trouble with SM58's, and for that matter most all live mic's, is that to sound good and to eliminate the feedback and bleed from other sounds on stage, you have to sing directly into them and hold the mic as close as you can to your mouth without actually eating it. But then your mouth is hidden, isn't it?

You can change that! Because it isn't about the mic at all. It's about the pre-amp settings before the signal gets to the soundboard. Boosting the gain on the pre-amp increases the sensitivity of the mic and allows the singer to sing away from the mic. Now the audience can see the singer's mouth! Problem solved! Sort of.

Increasing the gain in the pre-amp also increases the chances of feedback from monitors and sounds from the drums and amps. You have to meet with the house sound person before the doors open and ask them to try to find that fine line before your mic starts to feedback. The best way to get the house sound person to work with you on that is covered more fully in WAY #59.

And why not have your own mic stand as well? The ones that the clubs provide have seen better days. Buy a mic clip that allows you to slip your mic on and off easily. Spend some time on your home stage learning how to take the mic on and off the stand and to smoothly move the stand to the back of the stage when it's time for you to hold the mic in your hand. Practice that move at least 100 times until you can do it without taking your eyes off the audience or interrupting your patter. It'll look smooth and professional! Mic stand technique is a great visual – work on it!

Practice singing over the top of your very own mic so that the audience can see your mouth.

Eating the mic is a bad habit that you HAVE TO BREAK.

It ruins the visual of your delivery and performance.

Again, there is no reason anymore to spend the entire show with your mouth hidden behind the mic. Despite the solution described in the previous page, many artists continue to eat the mic, probably just from habit. **STOP IT!** Here's why.

There are a number of ways to communicate with your audience in which you can visually add emotion and meaning to the words and music of your songs. **The three main tools you have at your disposal are your hands, your eyes and your mouth**. It is important that the audience can see these three ways of communication at all times.

- **HANDS**: When playing an instrument, you need to set aside times where your hands leave the keyboard or fretboard and wave or clap in time or gesture or point at something going on that you want them to see.
- **EYES**: Keep your eyes open and on the entire audience, especially the ones in the back of the room. **And lose the pretentious sunglasses!** Even when you close your eyes and look away from the audience from time to time, you are communicating that you are feeling the song and perhaps they should be feeling it as well.
- **MOUTH**: Of the three, the most important is your mouth. That's where you convey the true meanings of your songs – are you happy, sad, sarcastic, bored or silly? Your mouth adds so much to the mix. And when it's a bad PA, they could still read your lips!

NOTE: Let me tout and/or apologize for my use of "mic" as the abbreviated or shortened version of "microphone" as opposed to the alternate spelling - "mike". Here's why:

1) I find that audiophiles use "mic" and non-audiophiles use "mike" and I tend to side with the professionals who actually use the damn things regularly.
2) My preference for "mic" also avoids the use of the phrase "eating the mike" in print.

**Get a tripod with
an iPhone holder**
attachment
to record your
rehearsals and
shows for critiquing.

**Forget about the
audio; this is about
the visual aspect.**

An iPhone on a tripod would work perfectly in the home or the garage rehearsal space you built according to my specifications previously in **WAY #39**. You could set up a feed from your cheap PA if you would like to hear how it sounds, but that would be best left to the song rehearsal time. **This is about the visual.**

Side note: The first band I was in back in Ohio used to rehearse in the rhythm guitar player's parents' living room. They had a huge wall-to-wall mirror hung above the fireplace and we would set up across from it and watch ourselves so that we could correct whatever wasn't working in real time. We tried filming it with a Super 8 camera but it took too long to get the film processed. And we found that there was a certain benefit in watching the show in real time that might have been lost on video; so if the iPhone camera idea isn't working for you, do the analog/real time thing in the mirror across the room.

Hire a **movement coach** to help you with stage presence, posture and performance style.

This isn't dancing - this is movement.

We're starting to get into areas now where you might need to call on some professional help. Up to this point, pretty much everything could be done and evaluated by you on your own, with minimum feedback or consultation from outside sources. And remember the rule from **WAY #7**: no input from family, friends or fans. They're not professionals and, even if they were, they're too close to you emotionally to give you honest feedback or help.

The areas where you've been able to call on professionals so far are pretty obvious - musical and vocal instruction, audio engineering, stylist - and now a movement coach. Call around to dance studios and ask if they have a course or instructor who specializes in stage presence and movement – not the same as dancing.

But next, you're faced with the specter of putting it all together (singing, playing, personality patter, movement, staging) into an entertaining live performance. Where do you get help on that? This would be an ideal time for you to check out my website:

http://www.diditmusic.com

Now is the time for you to consider taking the fast track toward stepping up your show to the next level - from performer to entertainer - by utilizing professional, experienced instruction. Lots more information at the website. I look forward to hearing from you.

#47 of 101 WAYS

Just because the way you wrote and maybe recorded a song works for listening purposes, **it doesn't mean that it's going to work live.**

Find the **"HIDDEN HEARTS"** in each song and rearrange around those parts.

It doesn't matter if YOU like the song. Of course YOU like the song – you wrote it and it's based on some personal experience and it's very meaningful to you. And you probably like the way you've arranged the song to please yourself and the potential listener. But the live audience is there for more than just listening – they want to be **ENTERTAINED**.

Repetition is how we learn. That's how an audience grows to like a song – hearing it over and over again. Other than playing a song twice in a row (which we used to do in a bar band I was in), you're pretty much stuck with making an impression with a song on the first listen. So what do you do? **You need to re-arrange the song from being listenable to being live.**

For instance, you could find **a memorable passage to repetitiously play** to an audience so that one listen is all they need to "get" the song. You're looking for a hook, a guitar lick, a background vocal, or a bridge – something that isn't obvious at first. **I call them the "HIDDEN HEARTS".**

Now let's go over three things that an audience may or may not enjoy about a hearing a song for the first time:
1) **FEEL.** How does it feel rhythmically? Up-tempo songs, especially shuffles, get an audience to nod their heads and tap their feet. They can't help it, so make it easy for them to do so. Add in the visual of you bouncing in time with the rhythm across the stage as you approach the mic, and you have their attention.
2) **MELODY.** If there's a catchy hook or **HIDDEN HEART,** get to it as soon as possible. Look directly at the audience as you sing or play that part. Make them notice it. Repeat.
3) **LYRIC.** Sadly, the part of the song that you as a songwriter think is the *most* important part of the song is the *least* important part to the audience on first listen. Your lyric, upon repeated listens, will take them to a new appreciation of the song, but not at first. First there's rhythm and melody. Accept that.

First you learn how to **perform the song.**

Then you work on **making the live performance ENTERTAINING.**

Two different things.

First you need to learn the song really well the way it was written and then re-learn it the way you've taken the song and rearranged it to make it more entertaining to a live audience as suggested on the previous page.

Sing and play the song over and over again until you can do it in your sleep, which is more or less the place you're trying to get to. You want to get to the point where you are not thinking about the lyrics, the chords or the **NEW** arrangement – you are only able to think about how you're going to bring an emotional delivery to the song and focus on the audience reaction to that.

Next you will want to address how you're going to **VISUALLY** make this song different from all the other songs in your set.

- Try moving the mic to the left or right side of the stage.
- Or maybe you go out into the audience and become a strolling guitarist or an *a cappella* un-mic'd troubadour for a verse and chorus?
- Sit on a stool or on the edge of the stage to sing your ballad.
- How about bringing some random audience member up on stage to play tambourine or bongos or some percussion? After all, everyone is a frustrated drummer.

Varying your presentation and location brings an element of surprise to your performance and each song becomes visually memorable as a result. By keeping the audience guessing as to what's going to happen next, you've made the show way more entertaining than it would have been had you chosen instead to stand in one place (i.e., center stage behind the mic stand) for the whole set.

Make up set lists
of one, two, three,
four, five and six songs.

That way you're
covered for anything.

**They may not be made
up of the same songs.**

In the course of your career, especially when you're first starting out, you will be called upon to perform song sets of different lengths because the events will exist for different reasons. You must plan ahead for such things and have set lists ready to go for all occasions. It's what **PROFESSIONALS** do. For instance:

1) **One song per artist on open mic night.** Which one should it be? I hope by now you know it has to be your best up-tempo song.

2) **Let's say you're at a songwriter round and each artist is doing two songs.** As long as the "audience" is fellow songwriters, then you can start with your favorite song (which is probably mid-tempo with a meaningful lyric) and follow that up immediately with your big up-tempo song. They're musicians – they'll get it.

3) **Three-song sets are popular when you're playing for a radio station or ad agency staffs at a conference room lunch show.** Start with your up-tempo number, go to your favorite mid-tempo and end with another up-tempo. Avoid slow, heavy ballads at such functions, especially during the daytime.

4) **Four is the best number of songs to demonstrate what you can do.** You should be able to show all of your strengths in four songs. Up-tempo, mid-tempo, slow ballad and end with a happy up-tempo.

5) **Five songs?** Two up-tempo numbers to begin with, then maybe a mid-tempo well-known cover, followed by your heart-wrenching ballad and end, once again, with the happy up-tempo number.

6) **Six is as many songs as you should do if you're an unknown artist to the audience.** Other than beginning and ending with an up-tempo song, include at least one cover and a ballad.

Also, be ready to do one more song at the end as an impromptu encore. To them, it'll be impromptu; to you, it will be all planned out. **Do not do the encore unless it is 100% warranted**. Be cool.

Structure your set lists just like books, plays and films: **a great beginning, a strong middle, and a memorable ending.**

An audience has paid good money to come to a club and sit (or stand) shoulder to shoulder with complete strangers and the unwashed masses for one reason: **THEY WANT TO BE ENTERTAINED**. They don't know that – they think they're there to hear you play your songs. But deep down, what they're really looking for is **ENTERTAINMENT** to take them away from their otherwise dull and dreary lives.

THEY WANT A SHOW. They want your set to have a little of everything – drama, comedy, music, spoken word, love, jealousy, danger, tension, surprise and, finally, release. That's why every song has to sound and look different from the others. You then need to arrange them in some sort of order so that there's a beginning, middle and an end. If not, then you're just throwing melodies, lyrics and rhythms up against the wall willy-nilly, hoping some of them stick. Some of them will, but certainly not all of them. Without forethought, cohesiveness, and orderly flow, it's not very **ENTERTAINING** and it's not a real show.

Think **THEATER**! You're putting on a play in six acts – one for every song in your set. And you need to introduce each of the six acts with some explanatory patter, unless you've already distributed programs (not a bad idea, actually). And all of the acts together form a complete program with a beginning, middle and end.

It's a tall order, for sure, and somewhat subjective as to how you would go about putting all of the pieces of the puzzle together. But you have to at least keep this thought in mind, this over-arching idea of the perfect set of perfect songs. Keep striving for that.

If you're an unfamiliar artist playing unfamiliar songs, your set should run **20 to 30 minutes. That's it.**

The contrary is also true: If you are an artist with whom the audience is familiar and you are singing and playing songs that are familiar to the audience, whether they're yours or cover songs, you can play as long as you like. Familiarity with you and your songs to an audience is definitely a career goal. You're not nearly there yet. You have to plan and work harder in order to get there. It's doable, but it'll take time and effort.

So, again, no matter how great you think your songs are or how well you've structured your set or how clever your patter sounds or how appealing you look, an audience who is unfamiliar with you and your songs are going to tune out at about the 20 to 30 minute mark. Besides, **if you can't do what you need to do to ENTERTAIN an audience in 20 to 30 minutes, then playing another half dozen songs in an additional 20 to 30 minutes is not going to win them over.**

Your goal is to prepare a **KILLER** 20-to-30-minute set of four to six songs with well-written, rehearsed and delivered patter in between each song and then say goodnight. (Have an encore tune ready, preferably a poignant ballad, but don't expect one, and don't be bummed if it isn't called for. **DO NOT FORCE AN ENCORE**.)

And don't try to cram as many songs as you can in the time allotted you. Leave room for patter and let the audience breathe. Let it flow.

And don't feel that you HAVE to fill up your 45-minute time slot just because that's what everyone else is doing. You can play your half-hour by starting late and ending early. The audience will enjoy you more and the club will have more time to sell drinks.

If the audience
knows your song,
play it as written.

If not, then
**keep rearranging
to make it better.**

This is not a hard and fast rule by any means, but a suggestion. If the audience knows your song for one reason or another well enough to sing along with it, then play and sing it as written – don't throw them off – they're enjoying singing out in a crowd and they obviously like the song. (Oh, and just because your mother and your friends know the song and are singing along, doesn't mean the rest of the audience knows it. I'm talking about people you don't know.)

However, if the audience doesn't know your song, there's no particular reason to play it as written or recorded. **There are certain "rules" one follows about how a song is arranged for recording, so that the song fits a format of a certain amount of minutes and such. These rules do not apply when you perform the song in a live performance.** As discussed previously, in a live performance, you can break the song down to its core and find the **HIDDEN HEARTS (WAY #47)** – the key phrase or lyric or melody or instrumental lick or harmony part or rhythm riff or whatever - and repeat it until it gets inside the heads of the audience.

Again, repetition is the key to memorable songs and to getting an audience to come back and see and hear you play that song again. Eventually, they may even sing along. Wouldn't that be a nice payoff?

Include a familiar cover in your multiple-song set and rearrange it to **make it your own**.

If you can't make it your own, then don't do it.

THE IMPORTANCE OF A COVER SONG: I cannot stress this enough. In a multiple-song set comprised of your unknown original material you must include a familiar cover song for a number of reasons. For one, the audience needs a break from your unfamiliar songs. It also allows them to hum or sing along if they'd like. **Perhaps they will even divert their attention away from their familiarity with the melody and lyrics to take notice of your musical inventiveness and vocal interpretive skills.**

The latter reason is key. Here is your chance to shine. You can be incredibly creative with the sound and the tempo of the song. You can make the previously simple chord progression more complex while still retaining the beauty of the original melody. You could start the song with the bridge and go right into the chorus even before you sing the first verse. Maybe you found a **HIDDEN HEART** in the song that was buried in the original production but has beauty; then you could make that **HIDDEN HEART** the centerpiece of your new arrangement and re-invent the song for the audience, showing them some alternative meaning they might have missed. As long as you keep to the original melody and lyrics, it's pretty much wide open. **That's what I mean by making it your own.**

However, if you remain married to the original version's arrangement and production, then you're just a cover band. That's not the path to a great career.

You could also do some background research on the original song's writer, artist or recording that could also shed some new light on the song for the audience. **Great set-up patter would be an added bonus.**

Develop a stage personality with an attitude.

Show it off in your between-song patter.

Presenting your musical work in an entertaining manner is the presentation of PERSONALITY. First, you need to have one – a personality, that is. And the best place to present that personality is in your essential between-song patter.

Up until now, you've probably not rehearsed anything to say from the stage and decided to "wing it". If you're going to do that, why even bother to rehearse your songs? Why not "wing" those too? Exactly.

I believe that the between-song patter is just as important as your songs (and could be even more entertaining). As such, it needs to be presented with the same amount of thought, preparation, and rehearsal as your songs. Entertaining patter leads the audience to a better understanding and appreciation of your songs.

You need to tell them stories between songs – things about the songs, about YOU and about THEM. The stories need to be short, as well as serious or funny or poignant, and they need to make a point. The idea here is to not only shed some light on the songs, but also how you FEEL about the songs, the world, relationships, music, and whatever else.

And make sure that you have three different stories for each song so when people come to see your show a second and third time, there's a good chance they'll hear different patter. THAT'S ENTERTAINING!

DO NOT ASK THE AUDIENCE HOW THEY'RE DOING OR IF THEY'RE HAVING A GOOD TIME OR NOT. Yes, I know that virtually all singer/songwriters inevitably say such things multiple times. But why should you follow in their trite and boring footsteps? Be original instead. What you have to say needs to be more than just some treacly, bland, or pointless thoughts thrown together. Write and rehearse something thoughtful, clever and ENTERTAINING! And while you're at it, please try to limit the number of times you thank the audience for showing up.

ALSO: You'll need to write and rehearse ten things to say while you're tuning up. Not meaningful things about your upcoming songs, but some zingers with punch lines. Time them out to match however long it generally takes you to tune up. Practice tuning up and delivering your zingers while looking at the audience. It's a trick to do, but it's also ENTERTAINING!

One way to make **an emotional connection with your audience** before and after your song is **through visuals.**

Most singer/songwriter/performers in my experience are certain that the best (and sometimes the ONLY) way to make an emotional connection to an audience is through the lyrical content and emotional delivery of their songs. Yes, that's true to a certain extent. But as I pointed out earlier, **the lyrics of your songs to an uninitiated audience take a back seat to the between-song patter and visuals** – the two things that are more readily identifiable to the majority of any audience outside of a music school.

Another way to communicate an emotion to your audience is by the visual cues you give that add gravitas to your song. Here's one example:
1) Once you've announced the name of the next song as a part of your pre-song patter, **back away from the mic stand or, if there's no room to back away, move off to the side** to a position where there is a clear sight line from you to the audience.
2) Close your eyes and start the guitar strum.
3) Then open your eyes and look up to your right – that's the side of your brain where you keep your emotions. Now the audience sees that you've left the personality patter phase of your show and that you are now entering the emotional state of the song.
4) When you're "ready," step in time to the mic and start to sing.
5) **Once the song is done, back away from the mic stand again. *Do not do or say anything.*** This shows them that the song has ended.
6) Close your eyes and look down. Wait for the applause to rise.
7) Then just as it reaches its peak and starts to drop, raise your head up, open your eyes and mouth a "thank you" during the applause. "Welcome back from wherever you went," they're thinking.
8) You can then step back to the mic and say a second "Thank you!"
9) Only then should you start to fuss with your tuning or take a swig of water or whatever – not before.
10) Quickly, you need to start your next piece of scripted patter, setting up the next song.

You will need to practice this a lot to make it believable. It works but only if you **use it sparingly.** Limit its use to your heavier songs. **NOTE:** If all of your songs are heavy, it's time to re-think your set list.

Make the

hard things

look easy

and the

easy things

look hard.

Here's a contradictory tip that I picked up years ago from being on tour with Van Halen. The audience would swoon when Eddie bounded across the stage, smiling and never looking at his fretboard, all the while playing one of the most difficult riffs imaginable and making it all look so easy. And then later, he would stand stage center and play some kind of Guitar 101 figure over and over again (loudly) while glaring at his fingers with a grimacing scowl as if he were really stretching out on this simple, repetitive trifle and, of course, the audience loved it.

He was making the hard thing look easy and the easy thing look hard.

Singers can pull off the same stunt. Be sure to make your most difficult song look and sound easy. And then also be sure to show the strain you're making to hit and hold some high note that we both know you could hit anytime, but the audience doesn't know that. Stuff like that.

Once again, I need to remind you that 80% or 90% of the average audience (I made that figure up, but it must be close to that) knows nothing about music or how to play or perform it. They're in awe of someone who has the courage to even get up on a stage, let alone to have the talent to perform as well. But they're not there solely to be wowed by your vocal or musical instrument facility; they're there to be **ENTERTAINED**. So put on a show for them. Remember the easy/hard tip.

Lose any appearance of pride on stage, even to the point of looking foolish.

Be vulnerable.

People love that.

"Until you're ready to look foolish, you'll never have the possibility of being great." - Cher

There are hundreds, if not thousands, of pieces of advice out there to the aspiring performer and entertainer. I'm only including a couple of them that seem counterintuitive, like the Eddie Van Halen example from the previous page and the edict from Cher above. **This is definitely one that you would never have thought of on your own. This one gets down to the essence of what I've found to be another major difference between performers and entertainers – and that difference is hiding behind your pride.**

I don't mean like the pride you take in your musical skills or professional standards. **I'm talking about the pride that everyone hides deep in their ego that prevents them from making fools of themselves in front of other people.** But there's nothing wrong with looking foolish on stage – as long as it's scripted and rehearsed and delivered with a wink. **That's entertaining!**

The audience holds a special regard for performers and entertainers for several reasons, not the least of which is that most of the people in the audience would be scared to death to get up on a stage and perform at all. But if you're playing it safe with your emotions and your show, then it's not so special. **The last thing you want an audience member to say is, "Hell, I can do THAT."** So it's incumbent on you to do or say some silly, rowdy, or foolish things that they would never consider doing anywhere – let alone from a stage.

The thing you have to get over is your reticence to doing something foolish on stage. **Show your vulnerability by letting that foolish pride go** – all successful entertainers have done so. Being vulnerable on stage is a great way to emotionally connect with an audience. If you can't (or won't) do that, be prepared to keep performing at the level you are now. As Cher says, "…. **you'll never have the possibility of being great."**

Once you're
good enough,
**play in front of
people whenever
you can.**
You'll need the
experience.

So what's "good enough"? Good enough not to embarrass yourself? Maybe, but be prepared to be embarrassed. **Live performance requires a thick skin. And here's where you to begin to get one.**

I often tell my clients to try to begin their performing career out of the limelight – out of town, if possible. If there's an open mic thing going on one town over, go there first.

No matter what, your first performances are going to be rough. Everything you do will seem amateurish, disjointed, stilted, contrived – all of the things you don't want to happen. **But it's like the first time you do anything that requires skill and experience. You have to go through that trial and error until you reach the place of experience and confidence.**

One thing for sure, don't get your hopes up or exude any false over-the-top bravado. It's probably going to be enough just to get on stage and get through a couple of songs without forgetting something.

And whatever you plan to do, plan to do it! Practice! Rehearse! Again, do not now or ever say to yourself, "Oh, I'll just wing it." **Winging it is for people who have been doing it (and doing it well) for YEARS. That's not you.**

EVERYTHING you do has to be planned and rehearsed from the way you walk on the stage to the way you walk off stage. If not, you're just setting yourself up for some embarrassment. Why would you want to do that?

Performance is not a fun thing at first – it's a job, and it needs to be learned, attempted, experienced, repeated and eventually done well. Once you've accomplished achieved some level of performance skill, then it's time to learn how to ENTERTAIN.

Before your show, befriend (and tip) the **club sound person**.

Ask him or her nicely to **play music before and after your set** that would complement your style of music.

There are certain protocols you need to be aware of when performing at the club level. A large club will have a house manager, production manager, stage manager, as well as sound and lighting people. In the small clubs one person will be doing all of those things. You must treat that person with the utmost respect. They have a lot of plates spinning at once and you are possibly and probably the plate about which they are concerned the least. Here are some guidelines:

1) **Show up on time. No excuses.**
2) It's OK to have one person to assist you, but only one.
3) **All of your gear must be in good working order.** Test everything before you leave home. Have extra batteries, strings and cords
4) **You probably won't get a soundcheck - maybe just a line check.** Sometimes even that line check will happen just before you are scheduled to go on.
5) If the sound or line checks are pre-doors, the headliner (or whoever is scheduled to perform last) will check first and whoever is going on first will check last. You may not be able to place any of your gear on stage until you perform.
6) There may be a house drum kit, upright piano and even an amp or two that the club would prefer you to use to speed up set changes. If possible, have all of your gear run through DI's (direct inputs).
7) **The ONLY thing you need to press for is to use your own vocal mic and mic stand.** I've never had a club sound person say no to that.
8) **Here is the most important off-stage thing that you will need to do, but you need to do it with some finesse.** Sometime before the show, when the sound person is alone and not really doing anything, you need to thank them in advance for helping you out and you need to subtly and professionally slip them a $20 bill. That doesn't buy you any kind of free pass to do or say whatever the hell you want, but it will somewhat ensure that you will get the best sound possible, that you probably will get him or her to cut you some slack, and that you will be remembered the next time you're there. In a good way.

Always have a visual representation of **your name on stage** – on a banner, on your guitar or keyboard, or even on your hat – **so that the audience will remember your name.**

How many times has someone told you about a singer/songwriter or a band they saw at some club last week and how wonderful he/she/they were, but they could not remember the name of the artist or the band? And even when you did a little research and came up with a possible list of artists that it could have been, they still couldn't tell you. Why not? It was because they had no **VISUAL** memory of the name.

Fortunately, that can be fixed easily enough with some kind of banner or sign or something with your name or easy-to-read logo on it that could be hung or placed unobtrusively at the back or side of the stage.

Or much like Chris Isaak and Elvis Costello early on, have your name emblazoned on the fretboard, front trim or back of your guitar. Or put your name over your keyboard's logo or on a bass drum head (The Beatles). Or silk-screened onto the dust cover or your amp.

Wait a minute, you say! That's HOKEY! True, it could be. But with some taste and creativity on your part, it can work. Get creative. **Figure out a way for your name to be prominently displayed while you're on stage.**

I vote for a banner that you can have made at FedEx or Staples for $20 on weather-and-wrinkle proof plastic with grommets across the top and bottom. Go for a white background with black, blue or red letters for copy or logo - something that can be seen and read easily from the back of the room. **No one will ever forget your name again.**

Get in the habit of **showing up on time or early for everything and be ready** to do what you're supposed to do.

"Eighty percent of success is showing up." - Woody Allen

If you want to be regarded as a professional, you will not only show up, you'll show up on time, early even. After all, what is it that you're doing the day of your important meeting or your show that's so much more crucial than your career? Let's go back to **WAY #1**:

"Make sure that MUSIC is the ONLY thing you want, need, and have to do in life to the exclusion of everything else."

Keeping that mantra ever in the forefront of your mind, you'll clear out your day and focus on not only showing up on time, but also prepared to discuss or do whatever it is you promised and are expected to do, and that includes putting on a great show.

Don't be "cool" – be punctual. Being late and lackadaisical is amateur.

SIDEBAR: The difference between an amateur (French for one who loves to do) and a professional (English for one who loves to make money at it) is that professionals have their act together, musically and businesswise. Amateurs then, by definition, are just having fun. Which is fine, as long as you're not bitter about no one being interested in paying money to watch you entertain yourself on stage. **Amateurs entertain themselves; professionals entertain their audience.**

The entire next section is all about becoming (or appearing to be) **PROFESSIONAL.**

PROFESSIONAL WAYS 62 - 82

The days of the music business putting up with amateur, inconsiderate, disrespectful, recalcitrant, unprofessional artists are over. You have to get your act together and be responsible and accountable for your actions (or inactions) from the start.

So next we have to take a long, hard look at your business. Because that's what this whole thing is – a business.

We're going to cover possibly changing your name, two books to read and memorize, who you're going to have to hire to look after your business for you, how to get set up legally and financially, signing up to all the pertinent income sources as well as a couple of online newsletters, gear insurance, media training, how to behave in public, why you should record all meetings and when to keep your mouth shut – stuff like that.

If your name isn't **star quality**, **change it**.

Make it easy to spell and pronounce.

Better yet: use one name.

Although the current affectation in the biz is to construct a stage name that contains no vowels and is so hipster that it cannot be pronounced, let's assume that there will be a return to normalcy where the audience doesn't have to waste time trying to figure out how to pronounce your name, allowing them to listen to the music.

But it is **REALLY IMPORTANT** that your name is also indicative of star quality and that it, at least tangentially, alludes to your style of music. For instance, if your given name sounds like you're the head of an accounting department*, maybe you should consider changing it. Here's how others have dealt with that problem:

Reginald Dwight = **Elton John**
(Elton likened his given name to the sound of a cement mixer.)
Stefani Germanotta = **Lady Gaga**
Elizabeth Grant = **Lana Del Rey**
John Stephens = **John Legend**
Katheryn Hudson = **Katy Perry**
Christopher Breaux = **Frank Ocean**
Robert Zimmerman = **Bob Dylan**
Carol Klein = **Carole King**
Peter Hernandez = **Bruno Mars**
Steven Tallarico = **Steven Tyler**
Mike Rosenberg = **Passenger**
Aubrey Graham = **Drake**
Ella Yelich-O'Connor = **Lorde**
Sonny Moore = **Skrillex**
Gordon Sumner = **Sting**

Bottom line: One name is best and if it's your actual given name, like **Cher** or **Madonna** or **Beyoncé**, all the better.

* Conversely, if you are the head of an accounting department and your name sounds like you're a member of a semi-famous speed metal band, then you, too, should consider changing your name to something more appropriate.

#63 of 101 WAYS

BUY and READ

Donald S. Passman's

<u>All You Need to Know
About the Music
Business, 9th Ed.</u>

BUY and READ

Randall Wixen's <u>The Plain
and Simple Guide to
Music Publishing, 3rd Ed.</u>

Don Passman's book, at almost 500 pages and now in its updated ninth edition, is the recognized standard of the industry. He covers all the salient areas you will need to know to be pro-active on certain things and not get ambushed on others. Of course, as a California attorney, he rightly and at several points in the book recommends that you seek legal advice from a qualified entertainment law attorney. But don't be intimidated by all that. Don writes in an easy, understandable style – no baffling legalese! https://www.amazon.com/Need-Know-About-Music-Business-ebook/dp/B00UDCl3RC/ref=sr_1_1?ie=UTF8&qid=1488872799&sr=81&keywords=don+passman+all+you+need+to+know+about+the+music+business

My side note on entertainment law: It's wholly unlike any other area of the legal profession. For that reason, **you should never seek counsel from an attorney who does not work solely in entertainment law.**

Randall Wixen's 200-pager is what I consider to be **THE** book on publishing. Not that Passman's book doesn't do a thorough job covering publishing in 120 pages or so, but Randall lays out some advice and opinions that you wouldn't normally find in a music business text. There are numerous other books on publishing that may be larger and so, you would think, contain more information. Nope. I've read them. This is the only one you'll need. https://www.amazon.com/Plain-Simple-Guide-Music-Publishing-ebook/dp/B00LZTEUOC/ref=sr_1_1?ie=UTF8&qid=1488863676&sr=8-1&keywords=randall+wixen

Warning! This is not to say that any book can cover the entire archaic, byzantine, contradictory, convoluted, and generally weird field of music publishing. You'll see.

You cannot do this alone — **you need a professional team and support staff** who know what they're doing and are passionate about you and your music.

"The industry is both the enemy and the best friend of the artist. Trouble is, they need each other." – Chrissie Hynde

Here's a simple breakdown of the people you will need (eventually) and the percentages that are pretty standard. Remember that everything is negotiable, if you are in a position to do so. Refer to the Passman and Wixen books for more detail, insight and strategy on the previous page.

Personal manager for 15-20%, but not until the point where you have something to manage.

Booking agent for 10%, except no booking agent will be interested in you until you can draw ever-growing crowds with your live show.

Entertainment attorney for 5% of your gross, although generally you can't get that deal without being signed to a major label.

Business manager for 5% of your annual gross, but not until you're grossing at least $50k/year.

Publisher for 10-15% domestic and 15-20% foreign to administrate your publishing.

A record company has the support staff (and funding) that you will need to get on the radio. They will take a varying percentage of everything you make. See **WAY #68** for alternatives to a label deal.

A Publicist/PR person generally works on a monthly retainer – anywhere from $500-$5,000. You don't need one, though, until you have something to publicize and promote, like your great live show! Find one who does all of their Social Media in-house.

Actually, once you start drawing crowds to your shows, **all of these people will find you**. And when they do, be sure to do your due diligence on each of them before you sign anything. At least use Google to dig up any past transgressions. Everybody has some.

Get an **FEIN** number online and stop using your social security number.

File a **DBA** with your local or state office.

Eventually you'll need an **LLC** to cover assets.

More business stuff: I'm fairly certain that about now your eyes are starting to glaze over and you're thinking about doing something else other than reading this because you hate the business side of the music biz and all you want to do is write and perform your songs and let someone else take care of the business, blah, blah, blah. **Stop it and grow up. This isn't that difficult.** It's actually pretty basic and, yes, at some point you will need others to take care of your business. You're not anywhere near there yet.

I'm sure you've heard or read the stories about all of the over-the-hill, down-on-their-luck musicians who are now living alone somewhere in a rented room with a drug and alcohol problem, blaming all of their troubles on some record company, agent, manager, publisher, or lawyer who screwed them out of their merch money/royalties/publishing. And how did that happen? **THEY NEVER LEARNED ANYTHING ABOUT THE BUSINESS AND WEREN'T PAYING ATTENTION WHEN IT ALL CAME DOWN.** Don't be that person. Read, learn, and pay attention!

OK, so first you'll want to stop using your social security number for business related things. Follow this link to the IRS website and get an FEIN number (Federal Employer Identification Number):
https://www.irs.gov/businesses/small-businesses-self-employed/apply-for-an-employer-identification-number-ein-online
It's meant for small businesses (like yours) that have employees. You don't have any (yet) but you're doing this to make sure that your social security number isn't floating around out there.

Next, apply for a **fictitious business name** with your County Recorder or Secretary of State office. It's also called a **DBA** (Doing Business As). Eventually you'll want to incorporate and get an **LLC** or the like, but that's really just to shield your assets and you don't have any (yet).

Get a **business license**, if required where you live, and then a **business checking** account where you bank.

Check with the city or county in which you live to see if a business license is required. It is in Los Angeles and Nashville. If so, apply for one.

Next, go to the bank where you have your personal checking account and open a business account. You'll need to have your DBA approval paperwork and your business license (if your city or county requires such a thing) with you as proof that you are a local, legitimate business. That way you keep your business revenue, payments and receipts separate from your personal funds. It's smart and professional. Or at least it looks that way. Your eventual business manager/bookkeeper/CPA will thank you and be duly impressed, if nothing else.

You'll be going at this alone for some time, so you might as well do it correctly and professionally right from the start. The cost is minimal and will pay off come tax time. **You *are* filing your taxes, aren't you?**

Sign up with **ASCAP** or **BMI** or **SESAC** as a writer and a publisher.

Join your local **Musicians Union.**

In order to sign up with a PRO (Performance Rights Organization) such as ASCAP (American Society of Composers, Authors and Publishers), BMI (Broadcast Music Inc.) or SESAC (Society of European Stage Actors & Composers), you'll need to record a song and put it up on CD Baby, Tunecore, Amazon, wherever, so that's it's for sale to the general public. You could have CDs made and sell them at your shows. You are now in the stream of commerce. Make sure that your song file metadata includes you as the artist, writer, publisher and record company.

Next you'll need to go to one of the PRO's and and sign up both as the writer and publisher of your song(s). There is a $50 application fee to join ASCAP (**http://www.ASCAP.com**) but BMI (**http://www.BMI.com**) is free to join. There are no dues for either one. You have to be invited to join SESAC (**https://www.SESAC.com**). As a result, they have a different set of rules but no dues or fees.

You'll need a name for your publishing company. Don't get cute. It would be best to name your pub something similar to your business name so that all your publishing business will match up name-wise with your DBA, your business license and your business checking account. Doing these simple things is a good start for you in the business world. Again, it looks professional and in the music business, perception is reality.

Joining the Musicians Union (the formal name is the AFM – American Federation of Musicians) is another step toward legitimacy (**https://www.afm.org/join**). AFM is for instrumentalists, of course, and those who accompany themselves for live shows – that's you!

The recently merged SAG/AFTRA (Screen Artists Guild/American Federation of Television and Radio Artists) is for vocalists whose recordings may be used in TV/Film/Commercials – could be you!

The AFM has annual dues around $200. SAG/AFTRA, however, is around $3k/year, but there's no real reason to join SAG/AFTRA until you have to. Don't worry - they will come to you and let you know when it's time. Eventually, you'll join both.

If you aren't signed to a label, you may still need help in the form of label services.

I recommend my friends at **www.theartistcooperative.com** - if you have the funding –

OR

http://www.indiehitmaker.com /dropkick-music-release- platform/

if you don't.

If you already have access to funding and have some music to promote and sell, you could get started by employing an independent music marketing and promotion company to provide all of the services that a major or indie label would supply but for a monthly fee instead of the labels' royalty and a percentage of your gross. **I highly recommend my friends at The Artist Cooperative.** Based in LA, with reps all over the US, they operate cafeteria-style, so that whatever services you need they can provide on a third-party basis and whatever you don't need, you don't pay for. **You can find out more about their services from my good friend Bob Divney through the website**: http://www.theartistcooperative.com

If, and what is more likely the case, you're short on funding, check out **Indiehitmaker**. Based in Atlanta, Bram Bessoff and his team help indie artists plan releases, find fans, build audiences, sell merch at their own speed by following a 12-step release plan, showing them how to run their own operation. Indiehitmaker also provides consulting services and products to help with team building and accomplishing goals. **Reach out to Bram to see if it makes sense for you.** He is very accessible and has a passion for helping artists. Find out more about their innovative and helpful Dropkick platform by going to:
http://www.indiehitmaker.com/dropkick-music-release-platform/

Which brings us to the nagging question of how do you pay the bills while you're working on your live show and your career? There are as many answers as there are singer/songwriters. But I'll state the obvious anyway: Try and find some subsistence job in or around the music scene – box office, bartender, craft services, promoter marketing assistant, sound or lights operator, stage hand. Try your hand at helping a venue book unknown or alternative acts on an off night – anything that gets you close to the biz and those who run it.

Get signed up to
SoundExchange.com

They track digital play and pay owners of sound recordings, as well as featured and non-featured performers.

And it's free to join!

There are four major countries in the world who do not pay performance rights royalties to recording artists or sound recording copyright owners (meaning record companies or whoever owns the master) for play on over-the-air radio: China, Iran, North Korea and, of course, the good old USA, where only the songwriters and publishers get paid for airplay.

As a step in the right direction, the Digital Rights Acts of 1995 and 1998 provide digital performance rights payments to sound copyright owners (that could be you), as well as to featured performers from sound recordings distributed digitally (that will be you when you've gotten to the level of performance acumen worthy of preserving your songs and vocals in media for distribution and sale to an unsuspecting public).

Sound Exchange is a non-profit performance rights organization that collects and distributes royalties on behalf of sound recording copyright owners (SRCO's – record companies, generally) and featured artists for non-interactive digital transmissions, including satellite, internet radio, and cable television music channels. Source: Wikipedia (And, yes, I donated to Wikipedia in a quasi-informal way for this use.)

https://www.soundexchange.com/

Sign up! It's free! And for fun, be sure to check out the list of artists to whom they owe money, although they can't pay any of them because, supposedly, the artists haven't signed up yet:
https://www.soundexchange.com/artist-copyright-owner/does-soundexchange-have-royalties-for-you/search-for-artist/
There is a Larry Butler on that list, but it's another Larry Butler.
I checked.

Sign up with **AARC** if you are the main performer or the sound recording copyright owner.

And it's free!

According to their website:

AARC (Alliance of Artists and Recording Companies) is the non-profit US royalty collective protecting the worldwide home taping (private copy), rental, and lending rights for featured recording artists and sound recording copyright owners (record labels). Although AARC is a US organization, it represents featured artists and copyright owners all over the world.

AARC provides a music royalty, generated by the sales of devices and media such as blank CDs, personal audio devices, automobile systems, media centers, and satellite radio devices that have music recording capabilities, to its participants worldwide.

Organized decades ago during the height of the home taping and music rental/lending scare, AARC still gets a royalty for every audio device, car system, home media center and satellite radio receiver manufactured and/or sold in the US. They then distribute those royalties through some secret black box computations to sound recording copyright owners (mainly record companies) and/or main featured artists – that's you!

Sign up! It's free! **https://wp.aarcroyalties.com/**

Get a **copyright** for all of your important songs that are getting actual attention in the marketplace.

There's a charge, but it's so worth it.

You don't really NEED to formally register all of your songs with the copyright office in Washington DC. Just the action of you writing down the melody and lyrics or recording them into your phone or putting your track up on Sound Cloud or iTunes technically makes it your song.

However, if there's a chance that your song might go viral or generate cover versions or get placed in a film, TV show or commercial (or show up on someone else's record), you'd better protect yourself with a copyright registration. It's the only thing that legally covers you when the ne'er-do-wells come out of the woodwork. And they WILL when they smell money. Before that, not so much.

And it's a pretty simple process. You can register your songs online and attach an mp3 file. If you do it online, it's $35/song, which is another reason you may not want to go to the trouble of formally copywriting ALL of your songs. You can copyright an entire album at once as long as you wrote and published all of the songs yourself ($55) but I think that one song at a time is the smart way to go in order to protect your most valuable songs individually. http://www.copyright.gov

NOTE: Even though you've registered online, it takes weeks, if not a month or so, to get the actual approval and paperwork back.

Copyrighting is not the same as registering your songs with ASCAP or BMI. A PRO registration won't do you much good in court, nor will the copyright registration entitle you to performance royalties. Two different things. **You should register your songs with both.**

#72 of 101 WAYS

Get listed with **Pollstar** –
for all the touring biz news

Subscribe to the
Bob Lefsetz Letter blog

Subscribe to the
Promoter 101 podcast

Find music and tech news at
Hypebot.com

Get the **ASCAP Daily Brief**
email blast

POLLSTAR is THE place to find out what's going on in the touring business and their live music industry database is second to none. Their annual Pollstar Live! February convention is THE place to meet everyone in the touring biz. You can submit your dates in advance by emailing them to Wendy at **tour_dates@pollstar.com.** In order to get your booking or management contact info into their directories, email Stephanie at **directories@pollstar.com** and ask. It's free to access their site and browse their charts, interviews and touring news, but in order to have access to all of their features and databases, it's $499/year for their Pro Online Only account. **http://www.pollstar.com**

THE LEFSETZ LETTER is THE Bible blog of the music industry. Bob Lefsetz is incredibly knowledgeable and passionate about popular music, the music biz and the people who run it, the media, and everything else in this internet-centric world we live in. Bob has an email fan base list that numbers in the tens of thousands. That way every reader can easily reply with support or to take issue with some of his positions. It's free! **http://www.lefsetz.com/lists/?p=subscribe&id=1**

PROMOTER 101 PODCAST – Emporium Presents promoter Dan Steinberg and Works Entertainment artist manager Luke Pierce offer up each week's touring biz headlines and in-depth interviews with music biz all-time legends and the legends-to-be. **http://www.promoter101.net**

HYPEBOT.COM – Hypebot is the leading music industry and technology news aggregator and blog hotspot published by Skyline Artists Agency head guy Bruce Houghton. Anyone can contribute to their Music Think Tank page for all to see. It's all free online! **http://www.hypebot.com**

ASCAP DAILY BRIEF - Compiled by ASCAP Board member, music publisher and songwriter Dean Kay (with assistance from ASCAP's Etan Rosenbloom), the ASCAP Daily Brief cuts through the media clutter to bring you links to the most relevant news and commentary on the rapidly evolving music industry and how it affects your future livelihood. **http://www.ascap.com/email**

Get insurance for your gear at **Music Pro Insurance**.

It's inexpensive - $150 a year covers $11k of gear including laptops.

First of all, let me say this in the clearest language possible:

IT IS INCREDIBLY STUPID NOT HAVE INSURANCE ON YOUR GEAR.

There.

Your first reaction is how expensive you think it is. It *is* expensive, if you try to add your guitar, amp, piano, PA, laptop, or whatever onto your renters or homeowners insurance as a rider. Ridiculously expensive.

But there's Music Pro. They're amazing! $150 a year covers up to $11,000 worth of gear and it goes up incrementally and gradually from there. They cover all musical instruments and related gear, including your laptop or whatever computer you're using. They do not cover phones and they don't cover wear and tear or electronic malfunctions. But I've had bands whose stuff was stolen and Music Pro reimbursed or replaced it all in short order.

And they offer accident and sickness insurance if you're travelling outside of the US. It's SO worth it. The keyboard player in a band I was managing had to have an emergency appendectomy while on tour in Paris. The Music Pro Insurance people took care of EVERYTHING including making sure that the doctor and hospital knew that there was coverage. And it happened over a weekend! In France! I love these guys.

If you do nothing else I've recommended in this book, do this one thing.
https://www.musicproinsurance.com/

Have a link on your
desktop and phone
to a file page of your
TOURING ASSETS INFO
ready to send to
club and concert promoters.

Include your headshots,
bio, video, music, tech rider,
stage plot and hospitality
requests along with your
management/agent/PR
contact information.

And keep it current.

Despite all of the fuss and furor about Facebook/Instagram, you should have an up-to-date, functional website. It doesn't have to do tricks or win awards or, worse, make the visitor jump through hoops to get to your vital information. It needs to have your current bio and tour dates and links to photos, videos and music and your social media sites. Pretty standard.

Plus you need to have a separate, stand-alone asset page. It will be a focal point of all of the things a club or concert promoter would need to help promote and market your show. You don't want to send out six separate email attachments to a promoter as you scroll frantically through your phone looking for your new photo or bio.

At the same time, **you don't want to overload the page either. Don't give them more than two choices of anything.**

1) Photos: headshots only, no long shots where you could be anybody. Two shots in color and two in black and white, one vertical and one horizontal.
2) Include a link to your most recent video and an mp3 of the song you're most known for.
3) You'll need to include a short bio, stage plot and/or mic/tech list.
4) You could add a short, sweet hospitality rider of only things you NEED not just what you want. Don't expect to get any of it, but it's OK to ask as long as you ask nicely.

Be sure to list the contact information for everyone related to your show. **Do not include any direct contact information for yourself. There are too many weirdos out there.**

Learn how to talk to the media well.

Get some **media training**.

You don't have to be nice – just be ready.

"Music journalism is people who can't write, interviewing people who can't talk, for people who can't read." – Frank Zappa

My own experience is that, at least in music interviews, there are only three questions from the media that you want posed to you:

1) Where have you been?
2) What are you doing now?
3) What are you planning to do next?

Everything else is unrelated to the story you want to tell. In real practice, however, dealing with the media involves so much more than being ready to answer the three stock questions above.

Do not think for an instant that the media are looking out for your best interests. It's a journalist's job to look for a story for their audience. The trouble is that it may or may not be the story you want them to tell. You may think that you're clever enough to stave off devious inquiries and steer all conversations into the message you want to deliver all on your own. You're not that clever. You need training.

Media training is a real thing. A person experienced in media pitfalls will teach you what to expect when subjected to media inquiries and situations. He or she will help prepare you with multiple stock answers and a planned patter of compliance or avoidance, so that you will be able to re-direct the questioning back to the three main topics listed above.

WARNING: Nothing is "off the record"; so be cautious and be careful. Get help. Google "Media Training" to find who's doing it near you.

#76 of 101 WAYS

The old adage of
KEEP YOUR PUBLISHING
until the time is right to
sign a publishing deal
is still true in pop & rock.

BUT IN NASHVILLE
there are a
LOT OF ADVANTAGES
in signing with a known
and respected pubco.

There are three well-worn paths to making money in the music biz these days – touring, merchandising, and publishing (although streaming revenue is positioned to become a much bigger factor in an artist's income later in this decade). Of the three, publishing is the long-term money. I could take up a couple of pages here listing reasons for the ins and outs of this piece of advice, but better yet, re-read the publishing section in the Passman book and/or the entire Wixen book as listed in **WAY #63**.

A great live act leads to touring, merchandising and publishing – **that's where it's at right now**. That's where long-term careers are made. All other ancillary revenue can be generated from the establishment of those three sources.

We'll get into touring and merch later; but for now, let's focus on your publishing. Initially, you will start out being your own publisher, just as you have been your own manager, booking agent, and publicist. Eventually, you will need to turn over all of that inside-publishing admin to a music publisher.

There are many advantages to securing a deal with a reputable publisher, especially in the Nashville community. There it is common for young, promising writers to receive a monthly advance, allowing them to focus on the writing process. Plus there's also the access to publishing professionals who, in turn, have years of relationships with record labels. **I can't say enough about the opportunities that exist in Nashville for young singer/songwriter/performers that exist nowhere else.**

NOTE: You should seek the advice and counsel of an entertainment attorney experienced in the field before you get into any kind of publishing deal. In fact, you should seek that very same advice and counsel for any deal with anyone about anything.

There are generally two types of song co-writing sessions:

Starting From Scratch
or
Sweetening Your Song

and each has its own **Preparation and Percentages/Splits.**

PREPARATION FOR A CO-WRITING SESSION STARTING FROM SCRATCH So you've somehow met up with a songwriter, maybe at a writer's round or through a friend, or perhaps you've read or heard about a songwriter and you did a cold call. Usually you will want to start with someone of a similar stature and genre as you; although it's always a plus to co-write with someone above your level of experience, talent and ability. At the same time, it's expected (at least in Nashville) that all songwriters should support the community by working with those who are less successful and experienced in order to teach them how to be better songwriters, just as others may have helped them in the past.

It's generally a good idea for the two of you to meet for coffee or tea (not drinks) to discuss histories, musical influences, and personal strengths (i.e., maybe you're better at melodies than lyrics). You might bring along some sample lyrics you've written or a phone recording of a melody or the start of a song. This initial meeting is designed to make for a better potential working relationship. If it isn't working, this might be the best time to determine that.

Assuming though that you two hit it off and plan a session, you need to gather up and organize your notebooks of song titles and lyrics and your files of melodies or sung phrases or whatever you have to get the song writing session started and moving along,

You two would then meet in whatever passes for a writing room - a rented rehearsal space, a recording studio, or, more often than not, whichever one of you has a comfortable and soundproofed room/garage/basement with few disturbances or distractions and an assortment of keyboards, guitars and gear.

PERCENTAGES IN A CO-WRITING SESSION STARTING FROM SCRATCH With from-scratch session co-writes, splits are historically determined by how many writers are in the room. Two? 50/50. Three? 33/33/33. If there's someone other than the two of you in the room, you need to discuss if the extra person is a contributor or not and if so, why. And if not, they need to leave or promise not to contribute. You don't want to lose a good chunk of your song to someone who blurts out two words without prompting. It's happened.

There are obviously advantages to writing with someone who already has hit songs and a publisher and/or a record deal, but you might have to (and should) give up a decent percentage to allow for that – maybe it becomes a 60/40 or even a 67/33. That *should* be discussed before the session starts and *must* be discussed by the time the session ends. Record the final decision on your phone.

Then there are the co-writing sessions where you want to sweeten your song that you've already written.

The Preparation and Percentages/Splits are somewhat different.

The Protocol's the same.

PREPARATION FOR A SWEETENING CO-WRITING SESSION If, indeed, you've already written most, if not all, of the melody and lyrics to a song (especially the chorus) and are just looking for sweetening, you should demo the song on your phone or Garage Band or something, along with a printed out lyric sheet, to take with you to the session to have available to play before you begin. That way you can establish up front that the song is already in an almost final form and that you're merely looking for sweetening and/or minor touches – a song doctor, if you will. Or you can be more specific, i.e., you're not completely happy with the bridge. **All of this should be discussed at the outset.**

PERCENTAGES FOR A SWEETENING CO-WRITING SESSION Keep in mind that, for the most part, **the melody and the lyrics are the only two major elements of a song that can be unquestionably copyrighted;** whereas grooves, chord progressions, drumbeats, guitar/keyboard/horn licks, harmonies, background vocals and "feel" **ARE NOT CONSIDERED TO BE MAJOR ELEMENTS** in a pure definition of a copyrighted composition ("Whiter Shade of Pale" and "Blurred Lines" notwithstanding). You **can** (and should) give up a percentage of your song to someone who adds an inventive chord progression or distinctive instrumental melody line – but how **MUCH** of a percentage is **YOUR** prerogative and not set in stone in some rule of law. **If you brought the majority of the melody and lyrics to the session, then you make the final decisions.**

What IS important is that you retain the controlling interest – 51% or more – of the composition. You want control the future use of the song. That way **YOU** decide the terms of any placements. **Be professional, be aware and be firm.**

THE PROTOCOL FOR BOTH CO-WRITING SESSIONS IS PRETTY MUCH THE SAME
Show up on time, maybe even a little early.
Shut off the ringer on your phone and do not check for texts or emails during your session. Only use your phone to record what you two come up with.
Have the whole day available. Start early and ALWAYS break for lunch.
Do not try to write a record – try to write a song. If it's a song, it'll be a record.
Don't ever criticize a co-writer's suggestions.
Don't be pushy – if your idea doesn't get a great response, drop it.
Be ready to compromise and make changes – that's what co-writing is.
No need to finalize everything right away. Come back to it after lunch!
When done for the day, re-establish percentages and publishing and copyright.
Plan a future for the song – who's going to demo it and what's the budget, etc.

#79 of 101 WAYS

Get a good recorder app on your phone to **record** meetings. Do not record telephone conversations without prior consent. There are laws against that.

If something is sent to you in written form and you don't understand it, you can consult with a professional as to what it means and/or you can go back to the originating party and ask for more detail or clarity. Either way, it's written down, so there's something somewhat substantial to go on.

However, when someone **says** something to you and you don't understand it, there's no easy way to seek counsel, so you have to ask for clarity then and there. Sometimes you get it and sometimes you don't. But either way, there's no document to back you up later, other than notes you may have taken (still a good idea).

This is why courts and depositions have reporters, to eliminate the gray areas of undocumented chatter and grandiose statements. In fact, I used to insist that a cassette recorder be present whenever my artists would do press interviews just so whatever they said would be reported correctly. I tried to introduce that same idea to other meetings and negotiations and was more often than not repudiated by those who apparently didn't want their verbal "agreement" preserved in any form.

These days I'm finding it easier to introduce a recorder to a meeting or negotiation thanks to the recorders on our phones. You can use the built-in software, but I would suggest you look around for a version that might have some neat transposition and/or document-share options.

You can record a phone conversation with one of the fancy models, but you HAVE to get permission from the party at the other end.

Even if you're not actually recording the meeting or conversation, at least say you are and take notes regardless. My experience is that people will watch what they say way more carefully and make fewer idle promises if they think it might be played back at some point. Beware the ones who absolutely reject the idea of recording their business conversations or meetings. They're up to something!

Don't complain
to anyone
about your
perceived problems
with the current
state of the
music business or
the people in it.

"All that jealousy and aggravation and spite. What you should be doing (instead) is working on whatever it is you . . . do. All that energy you're putting into saying, 'Where's mine?' Try putting that energy into the other thing." – Marc Maron, WTF podcast, Episode 731

No one wants to hear your diatribe about how awful things are and how the system is "rigged" against you or how the general public wouldn't know good music if it bit them in the ass, or how wonderful it used to be, etc.

There's never been a "wonderful" time to be in the music business. Even when vinyl and CDs were flying out the door, there were still the golden gates into record companies that needed to be pried open.

There will always be something "wrong" with the system, but the artists who have the passion to try to make something happen (and also happen to luck out and do well) will do so even during the downturns in the economy and the various "bad" musical climates.

And if you don't have the answer today, wait until tomorrow – something will happen, something will change. Maybe not for the better, but change brings new opportunities.

And for God's sake, lay off any backbiting you might have about your sense of entitlement and how come you're not a star and the other guy is. Or how this guy screwed you and stole your rights or any other perceived "wrongs" that you've been dealt.

Quit bitching about it and instead spend that energy doing whatever it is that you want to do and can do to further your career. If you're persistent, your time will come. It may not be tomorrow, but it will come. And if it doesn't, at least you tried. Shut up and get busy.

Do not speak loudly
in public places -
bars, restaurants and
especially elevators.

Do listen in on
other peoples'
conversations
for song lyrics.

You never know who's standing or sitting next to you or, worse, within earshot, in most public places. Such situations are ripe for giving up your good ideas or potential deals inadvertently to someone nearby, someone who may have the means to run with it now while you're still talking it through. **So keep your voice down!**

The reverse side of that is YOU should listen in on all the conversations you can in bars, restaurants and elevators for song lyrics or ideas. What are the real travails of real people and what would their lives sound like in song? Don't limit yourself to songs about **YOU** – write songs about **THEM**. And what better way to find out what's really going on in someone's life than to eavesdrop on a private conversation? Thanks to the ubiquitous public cell phone conversations these days, there's plenty of material out there.

"When you try to write dialogue, you get lots of clichés, don't you? But, when you ride the Tube, every line you overhear people say, it all sounds original. People are naturally original." – Richard Russell, head of UK's XL Recordings

Do not write, email, text or record anything that could be used against you in a court of law.

You may think that the slightly jaundiced email/text/Facebook post you just sent to a colleague is funny, but maybe it won't seem so funny in a libel suit. It happens all the time. In the past, paper letters and notes would be thrown away or destroyed; now digital transmissions live on practically forever. Even if you and the recipient delete the offending screed from your laptops, tablets or phones, it still lives in a server somewhere, waiting to be retrieved by plaintiff counsel and presented to you in a deposition.

If you feel that you have to express some vindictive diatribe, if you're planning on not following your contractual agreement to the letter, or if you're laying out plans to do something scurrilous, better to do so directly to the party you want to tell it to, verbally and in person, and be done with it. No voice mails, please.

I'm not saying that you would even think of doing anything like whatever it is that I'm alluding to. Just don't write it down or preserve it in any medium regardless.

TOURING

WAYS 83 – 92

OK, as discussed before, until you have a proven, killer live show and an ever-growing audience to back up that claim, you have no business being on tour. If you're having trouble drawing crowds in your hometown, what makes you think that it's going to be better somewhere else?

Still and all, what would a treatise on live performance be without some sort of section about touring? So what follows is a reality check about the vagaries of touring. We will start with an unglamorous warning about touring in general, why touring regionally makes way more sense to start with, and a warning to avoid all outside shows, particularly if your stage time is during the day.

Most importantly, I've included seven of my hard-learned **Rules of the Road** that offer essential tips to those who choose to ignore my warnings and go out on tour anyway.

Touring is a lot of long, boring days of uncomfortable travel interspersed with the occasional half-hour or so of stage time high.

Touring is not at all how it's presented in the movies and TV – it's not nearly that much fun and they leave out all of the boring parts. But since you're a singer/songwriter/performer, your performance skills define who you are, and so you must, at some point, go out on the road. It's probably a little early in your career path to discuss the specific ins-and-outs of touring, inasmuch as you need to conquer your hometown first; but there are realities and pratfalls ahead and you might as well get to know them now.

I've included these tips in the **101 WAYS** because I've found that touring (and recording an album and making an expensive video) are, at least in the minds of novices, the three most important things they need to do in pursuit of a career in music. Newbies believe that they need to do these things before anything else and the sooner the better, despite the costs and no foreseeable returns on investment.

In reality, they are the LAST things you should be doing. You need to be ready, I mean *really, really* ready, before you take on any or all of these juggernauts. They're time consuming, costly and frankly embarrassing if you're not ready. Your show, your songs and your visuals have to be the best they can be before you try to tackle these beasts.

The only difference among them is that both recording an album and making an expensive video can be fun (and revealing) but touring is no fun at all. And they're all three very expensive.

That being said, let's examine some thoughts on touring.

First conquer your zip code and hometown. Then branch out regionally or multi-state. Then maybe even your time zone.

Your eventual goal is a Top 20 market.

It's pointless, fruitless and money down a rat hole to suddenly take advantage of some windfall touring opportunity when you haven't yet secured a local or regional rabid fan base. **Fan bases grow from word of mouth** – your stellar performances encourage attendees to come back the next time and bring their friends. Then when you get a gig in the next town over, a portion of those people will follow you or at least let their friends in that town know about you. And that's how it grows. It's all about being great and repeatedly playing out. **Talent and repetition are the keys.**

Even if you happen to secure some third-billed touring gig with some popular headlining friends of yours and you've managed to get your show up to snuff, you're still an unknown in those towns AND there's little to no chance of a repeat performance. Don't do it. If you're that good, the chance will come up again.

This doesn't necessarily apply if your reputation precedes you – perhaps in the form of solid radio play or some viral YouTube video. However, **if the audience already has some knowledge as to who you are, your show will have to be even better than expected.** First impressions count for a lot. If your show isn't ready and the ones who show up to see you come away disappointed, they will write you off for good. And they'll tell their friends, too.

At some point, and you'll know when, your show will get up to par with the big boys in a nearby Top 20 market. Then that's where you will need to move to in order to get access to the opportunities of a big market and attract attention of your future team members. That's where they live; go there. If you already live there, go build your reputation elsewhere first.

Avoid outside gigs

It's too difficult to make a connection with an audience when outside.

The production is never as good as inside.

And then there's the heat and the cold and the rain and the bugs.

It's hard enough to establish an emotional connection with an audience inside, even when you're lucky enough to have all of the advantages of great production available to you.

But all of those essentials of communicating with an audience are lost whenever you go outside, especially during the daylight hours. The audience can't see you (too far away and the glare of the sun), they can't hear you (sound does strange things when you add wind), and there are too many distractions (birds, planes and cloud formations, to name three). Extreme cold and heat (not to mention rain) do bad things to guitar strings and amplifiers.

Besides, meaningful songs should not be performed during the day, especially outside. You need to have the full attention of an audience to pull off a song with lyrical meaning, particularly if the song is unfamiliar. Even the smallest, rattiest club is preferable to outside. I contend that artist/writer/entertainer genre works best at night in the dark confines of a venue with just enough alcohol to take the edge off.

Now, as a public service, I've listed seven pertinent Rules of the Road culled from a much longer list. Ignore them at your own peril.

#86 of 101 WAYS

Rule of the Road #1

Assume nothing.

Always call ahead.

Everything changes.

Double check – twice!

You will never be
sorry you did.

Don't fall into some sort of false confidence that everything you've painstakingly planned down to the last detail will go off without a hitch. You have to allow for the inevitable **HUMAN FACTOR** and what's known in the touring trade as **FORCE MAJEURE**, a French term found in most performance contracts, which means that liability can be waived when faced with certain unforeseeable circumstances, i.e., weather, wars and acts of God. Even then, many of those problems can be averted if you would just call ahead and double check everything.

Then there's also the fairly obvious stuff:

- Just because your plane is scheduled to leave at noon, that doesn't mean that it's actually going to leave at noon. Get there early regardless.
- Just because the morning hotel desk clerk assured you of a late checkout later in the afternoon, that doesn't mean that the afternoon clerk knows anything about it (and, of course, the hotel manager has gone for the day).
- Just because your soundcheck is listed on the original production schedule as set for 3:00 sharp, doesn't mean that's still true two weeks later. Call and ask. Nicely.

NOTE: And when the people you call get *irritated* at your insistence on double-checking, you should calmly suggest a few ways in which their lives could be *improved* by the addition of this rule.

Rule of the Road #2

Eat whenever you can.
Avoid all local cuisine.

Eat the same food
for every meal.

The Ramones would
try to only eat pizza.
Seriously.

One of the reasons people burn out on the road is that they don't eat when they should – and you should eat whenever there's food available. Do not believe the idle promise that everyone's going to dinner at some great place later; it probably won't happen**. If there's food available and you have 20 minutes, eat it now.**

Here's something I learned while out on tour with the Ramones. They had found that it was better to eat only one kind of food while on tour so as not to produce any gastro-intestinal problems that inevitably occurred on overnight bus trips when one samples the many varieties of regional foods encountered on cross-country tours.

In determining which one food should be consumed at all meals, here were the Ramones' criteria:
    1) Something that's the same all over America,
    2) That can be ordered (and delivered) 24/7/365, and
    3) That keeps its taste and consistency for hours (even overnight) without any refrigeration.

That food, of course, was pizza. That's primarily what they ate on tour. Think about it. It's food for thought. Sorry.

Rule of the Road #3

Sleep whenever you can - there may not be a chance to later.

Take a 20-minute nap when you can.

Try the "Coffee Nap".

According to studies in the UK, the key to staying alert during the day isn't a coffee *or* a nap; it's coffee *and* a nap, or colloquially, a "Coffee Nap". Here's how it works: First drink a cup of strong coffee. Second, take a 20-minute nap. Finally, wake up feeling refreshed and energetic.

You have to understand how caffeine affects you in order to accept this plan of action. After caffeine passes into your bloodstream, it crosses into your brain. There, it fits into receptors and does it job, UNLESS those receptors are already filled by adenosine.

Adenosine is a byproduct of brain activity, and when it accumulates at high enough levels, it plugs into these receptors and makes you feel tired – apparently from too much thinking. But if the caffeine gets there first and blocks the adenosine, the caffeine defeats the tiredness. Now, caffeine can have a hard time trying to block every single receptor because it has to compete with the adenosine for these spots, filling some, but not others. Caffeine can only fill up the receptors that aren't already occupied by adenosine. Ideally, you want the caffeine to arrive in the brain when the receptors are empty and available, which is when you aren't tired.

So here's how the Coffee Nap works: It's all a matter of timing (isn't everything?). Sleeping naturally clears adenosine from the receptors. Experts agree that a 20-minute nap is ideal. And, coincidentally, it takes around 20 minutes for the caffeine to get through your bloodstream to your brain.

So, drink some strong coffee before your 20-minute nap. That nap will reduce your levels of adenosine, opening up the receptors in 20 minutes, just in time for the caffeine to kick in. The caffeine will have fewer adenosine molecules to compete with, and will therefore make you alert. **Admit it: you've never tried it. Just try it.**

#89 of 101 WAYS

Rule of the Road #4

Always have your own transportation. Either you drive or make sure there will be a taxi/Uber/Lyft. Never depend on anyone else.

Never ride with someone else if you have your own car; make them ride with you. Never go anywhere if there's no taxi/Uber/Lyft available to take you back. **If you do not follow this rule, you will be stranded with the Van Halen band and crew at a low class strip bar in The Middle Of Nowhere, Texas, at three o'clock in the morning with no way out.** It happened to me; something similar could easily happen to you.

Rule of the Road #5

Never eat, drink, smoke or take anything without knowing what's in it.

If someone says, "Don't worry. It's fine," then you *know* not to.

This is something that I assume your mother or other adults have already tried to tell you but you wouldn't listen, would you? At some point soon you're going to have to say to yourself, "Oh, yeah – that's right. That was Larry's **Rule of the Road #5!** Why didn't I listen?"

Rule of the Road #6

Always get a receipt –
a printed receipt.
**It doesn't matter
what you actually *do*,**
as long as you get a
printed receipt
for reimbursement
or tax purposes.

Start practicing this habit now. First, get a receipt for everything you do, even if you don't believe that it has anything to do with your career. Try and devise an unconscious habit of placing all receipts in a wallet or purse or something that you always carry with you that closes securely. Avoid sticking receipts in your pockets or leaving them in bags or on the floor, trunk or glove compartment of your car.

Do not rely on your credit card statements for this because by the time the statement reaches you, you will have forgotten why you made the purchase AND the IRS doesn't regard line item credit card statements as proof – only proper receipts.

Each evening, pull out each receipt, circle the date and the amount and try and come up with a reason why it relates to your career. Put them in a monthly envelope and forget about them until tax time. Then you and your tax person can go through them and determine which ones are viable deductible items.

You will NEVER regret making this a habit because it's all about the money.

Rule of the Road #7

Nothing is definite until after it happens.

Even then, it might still be open to interpretation, but at least it'll be over.

Here are a few examples of the idle promises you'll be handed on tour. Memorize them and recoil instantly when someone says them to you.

The gig is all set for next weekend. No worries.
It's a small guarantee but everyone goes into percentages.
You will be listed in the club ad and on their website.
There's just you and two other acts on the bill.
There's always plenty of parking on the street and they don't tow.
You'll have lots of time for a soundcheck.
It'll sound great once the people get in here.
The catering is on its way.
Doors open promptly at 7:00, and you'll go on at 8:00 sharp.
We'll do a good walk-up.
All of this mess will be cleaned off the stage by the time you go on.
Everyone who's anyone is coming to your show.
All of the names are on the guest list plus one.
We'll hold tables for the agents and A&R people you've invited.
That noisy ventilation fan will be shut off while you're on stage.
Your stuff will be safe in the dressing room.
The club will have someone to sell your merch for you.
We enforce a no-talking rule while the performers are on stage.
You'll have loads of time to pack up after the show.
The garage stays open after midnight.
We've never had any problems with the fire marshal.
I'll have the cash for you by the end of the evening.
This check is good.

All of these idle promises were made by people who knew that if they didn't actually happen as promised, it would be too late for anyone to do anything about it.

MERCHANDISING

It's time to add another team member - a **merch person.**

OK, not much to say here – it's all pretty self-explanatory. Merch is a necessary evil to live performance as it **CAN BE** a revenue source if done well and micro-managed.

However, if there's one thing that can be more trouble than it's worth in the early stages of your career, it's merch. But you have to have it for cred and, when done right, it's the difference between making money or not on a "paying" gig.

You really can't rely on the club or promoter rep to do a great job but leaving your merch unattended while you're on stage has never seemed like a good idea to me. So you're going to need a separate person to deal with it. **But anyone can do merch, right? Not right.**

The hard part about getting and retaining a merch person is not only do they need to be trustworthy (**there's money involved** after all), but also the job is out of the cool action (vis-à-vis the audio engineer, musical accompanists, tour manager) and as such, **there's not a whole lot of glamour attached.**

And, to make the position even harder to fill, this person needs to exude personality and sell stuff! You may have to pay them a percentage of sales. It's the only way to attract someone who can do the job well. **And you need to have someone do it well.**

I'm not going to get into the duties and inside tricks of selling merch – there's plenty of information online about that. I do have some thoughts about the creative process, inventory and logistics of merch, to be found on the following pages.

Be sure that
your name and logo
are on your merch
and they can be
**legibly read from
20 feet away -**
without squinting.

There's a lot to be said for just slapping your name or logo in some large and legible font on everything and making it available in a variety of colors and be done with it.

There's no need to get fancy. Avoid freelance designers; by definition they will produce something "artsy-fartsy" that can't be discerned by the untrained eye. **You do, however, want to utilize someone experienced in graphics production;** just don't give in to anyone's weird designs.

What you're aiming for here is free branding. You want the unsuspecting fan to buy a wearable that they'll actually show-off in public for some time, kind of like a free sandwich board, or more current, a sign spinner. The thing is, you want other people to be able to read your name from some distance, so they don't actually have to stop the wearer and ask, "What the hell does that say?" Some will do that; most won't.

Place your merch with an **on-demand merchandise site.**

Only carry samples.

Eliminate inventory and leftovers.

Like everything else you're doing now, merch is an investment up front. You need inventory to show and sell. Of course, the problem with selling things that come in sizes – T-shirts, hoodies and such – is that at the end of the year, you're stuck with the designs and sizes no one liked. The trick then is to only have things that sell and yet have a variety of items, but nothing that takes up too much room in the trunk of your car. Good luck.

The best way to get around the wearable inventory problem is to utilize one of the many merch-on-demand sites for fulfillment. Google on-demand merch and read the reviews. You should have one of everything for display purposes and maybe a few on hand for those fans who just HAVE to have something NOW (do it hush-hush and charge extra).

As far as the smaller stuff – hats, pins, CDs – you should have plenty on hand. They're easier to store and replenish and you'll only have a little left over at the end of the year.

SOCIAL MEDIA WAYS 96 – 98

OK, here's another ancillary to your live show and career. This one, however, has replaced a large and expensive area (advertising, marketing, publicity and promotion) with a not-so-large but still somewhat expensive area that addresses those very same topics, but with far fewer personnel required to do all of those things.

The best part about Social Media is that it can even be encapsulated down to one person – a Jack/Jill-of-all-trades and a many-hats-person to be sure – but one person is now doing all of those things at many levels of the biz these days. However, some caveats are needed and they take up the next few pages.

Get an
**online marketing
person** who can
write code
and also be an **IT
trouble-shooter**.
Triple threat!
So valuable.

Here we go again – building the team, one position at a time. You'll need help and support to get your operation off the ground. The next step is to fill the Social Media position. So important.

The trick with social media is that it's difficult to determine if whatever it is that they're doing is actually accomplishing anything (as compared to, say, an audio tech or merch person), which is an inherent problem with the whole online marketing aspect of everyone's career. Of course you have to remember that a lack of followers and fans **COULD** be a result of whatever **YOU'RE** doing (or not doing) as an artist/writer/entertainer. A social media marketing person's job is to **CONVEY** the message of your music as well as the reviews and accolades of your entertaining songs and shows to a fact-starved fan base - not to **MANUFACTURE** fans for you. Be ready to have that discussion and own up to it.

Two added skills you should look for in this hiring (and you're going have to pay something to this person no matter what, if you're expecting to get results) **would be some IT knowledge and coding experience.** You're looking for someone who LIVES AND BREATHES every aspect of the social media spectrum.

What we're up to here is to get all of the areas up and running that a manager/agent/attorney won't want to deal with anyway. Without this support team building your foundation, you won't be ready when the big dogs enter the picture. And you need to be ready.

Keep in touch with your **SUPERFANS,** but not too much.

Stay current and be informative, but **keep the mystery** by peeling back the onion.

Play to your devoted, dedicated fans, but avoid any unclear, inside references where a casual observer might feel left out. Do not try to play to the masses with a wide-reaching, generalized, press-release-sounding spiel. It must feel intimate, cool, smart, and personal; and at most, a call to action. Give your fans some credit for being able to think and decide to do what is right for them.

Consistency is key and therein lies the conundrum – how often is often? You need to be fresh and current, but not inundating. I know you want to be sincere and wait for the right thing to come along to say, and to do nothing until you feel like it, because then it will feel like it's real. But are dealing with your songwriting in the same manner – you know, only when you feel like it? That's a lovely artistic thing to do and a career stopper.

Generate posts even when you don't feel like it.

Write songs even when you don't feel like it.

Practice/sing/play/perform/entertain even when you don't feel like it.

I happen to believe **social media is for fan interaction and calls to action**.

Keep the tickets, CD sales and merch on the website.

#99 of 101 WAYS

YOUTUBE

Get a YouTube page
and get in on monetizing
your music there
by clicking on this link:
**http://www.hypebot.co
m/hypebot/2015/10/ho
w-to-monetize-your-
music-on-youtube.html**

TV/FILM/ADS

TV/film/commercial song placements are made by those who have personal relationships with music supervisors and ad agencies.

If you don't have those relationships (and why would you?), you need to find someone who does, and there's the trick. Music placement people are the 21st century version of song pluggers. The best way for you to get the opportunity to work with someone who really has those relationships is for you to make music that fits into the format needs of each of the three main media: TV, film, and commercials.

And what are the needs of each of the three formats? Here are my thoughts: **TV wants innocuous music that does not take anything away from the scene; film is looking for complementary, meaningful music to make the scene better; and commercials want to make sure that the music doesn't get in the way of the audience remembering the product. Good luck.**

Next and more often than not, **the real decision maker is not the music supervisor - it's the film director, series show runner, or ad account manager.** These people may know nothing about music, so the music supervisor has to convince that decision maker to go for your song based on something other than the music itself. My experience is that you have to have some cool cachet (local gig buzz, playlist slots, local radio airplay) to get the OK. **So work on your local gig buzz!**

Even then, the music supervisor is expected to present anywhere from three to five songs (or more) to the decision maker for approval. To even get on that short list, **the determining factors will be: how fast, cheap and easy will it be to get all the rights cleared for this song**? Does the artist own the song and the publishing 100% or at least have control of the composition? Does the artist own the master outright? Is the artist open to negotiation? At the end of the day, given that all of the music choices are equally viable, it will all boil down to those three questions.

And so, all too often, the song that is the easiest and the fastest to clear will be the one that gets picked. That is all the more reason for you to be a solo artist/writer/entertainer – one who owns your own songs and recordings. You could become a music supervisor's new favorite artist for those reasons alone. Ka-ching!

SOLUTIONS

Studies show that creative artists have **more emotional problems** than the average person.

Solution? **Seek and accept help.**

"Keep your overhead down, avoid a major drug habit, and play in front of other people every day." – James Taylor

If you plan to become a successful artist/writer/entertainer, advice from James Taylor would be as good a place as any to start. Not that James actually did any of those things early on. He learned those lessons later in his career, but soon enough to recover and steady the ship. But you could save yourself ten years or so of turmoil by heeding his words from the get-go.

Creative artists' lives are, fairly frequently, ruled by their emotions, which take undue precedence over rationale, reason and reality. James himself sought help while still young, spending some time in various hospitals searching for answers for his ongoing depression. He got hooked on heroin, but managed to overcome his addiction in his 30s through a 12 Step program. You could copy his story, but no two people's lives are the same. Follow your own path.

We have all heard that drugs and alcohol are considered to be the shortcuts to creativity. But they're also the express lanes to dysfunction. And don't think you're immune – you're not. It's not about having any will power or common sense or not. It's way more serious than that.

And addiction goes beyond the poster children of alcohol and drugs. There's nicotine, caffeine, antibiotics and Afrin, for instance. They're all good in moderation, but moderation is not a common attribute of artist/writer/entertainers.

There are solutions and there is help. Search out someone who has suffered through many of the same problems as yours and could offer some suggestions. And when help is offered, accept it. Seek and accept. It's the only way out.

FINAL NOTE

LUCK AND OPPORTUNITY FAVOR THE PREPARED

It all comes down to being in the right place at the right time with the right skills and talent to back it up.

All you can do is to keep at it and

DON'T GIVE UP!

ABOUT THE AUTHOR

Larry Butler has devoted his entire life to the live performance side of the music business. He played keyboards and guitar in bar bands in Ohio during high school and college, serving as band manager and booking agent, followed by stints as club booker/manager and concert promoter.

He then moved to Los Angeles to begin working as a tour manager for such artists as Randy Newman, Ry Cooder and Isaac Hayes. Those efforts led to a job at Warner Bros. Records as VP Artist Relations, spending 20+ years touring with an unrivaled roster of talent, resulting in a couple of Pollstar Artist Development Executive awards. Although the focus at WBR was to utilize touring to sell records, Larry also coached many young artists in performance, staging and media relations. He left WB/Reprise to join Bill Silva Management as General Manager where he also was the day-to-day for Jason Mraz's publishing.

Larry now heads up his own Did It Music, based out of Nashville. His focus these days is on teaching young singer/songwriter/performers the steps that lead to becoming true artist/writer/entertainers. His first book, *The Twelve Lessons of Rock 'N' Roll*, is also available in digital and in print. And there's a Twitter feed – **@larryfromohio** – where you will find a different quote each day from famous artist/writer/entertainers about their music and performing experiences. And please feel free to post your positive comments and likes at his Facebook page **@LarryButlerLivePerformanceCoachAuthor** as well as the Did It Music Instagram page: **@diditmusic**. The website is at **http://www.diditmusic.com**.

INDEX

THE SINGER/ SONGWRITER RULE BOOK

101 WAYS

TO HELP YOU IMPROVE YOUR CHANCES OF SUCCESS

Made in the USA
Columbia, SC
10 July 2018